To Sean,

Thank You!

12/31/09

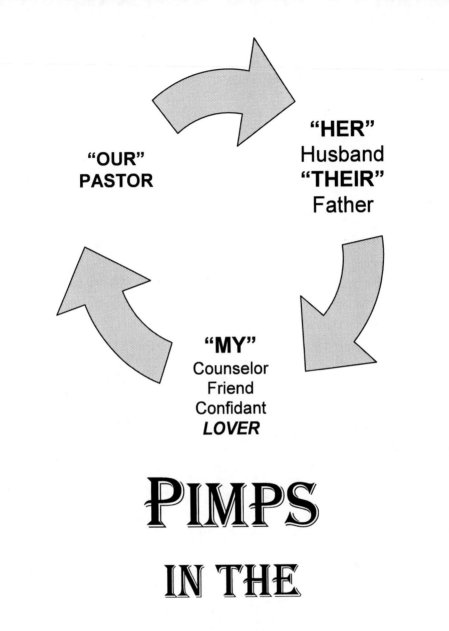

"OUR"
PASTOR

"HER"
Husband
"THEIR"
Father

"MY"
Counselor
Friend
Confidant
LOVER

PIMPS
IN THE
PULPIT

PIMPS

IN THE

PULPIT

PIMPS

IN THE

PULPIT

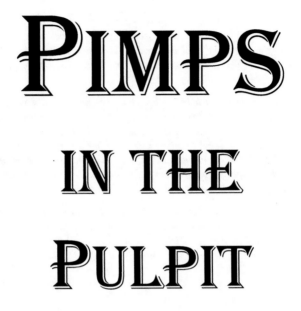

**HE WAS MY...COUNSELOR,
FRIEND, CONFIDANT AND LOVER,
"HER" HUSBAND, "THEIR" FATHER
AND OUR "PASTOR"!**

Shannon R. Bellamy

Shannon Bellamy in association with

INFINITY
PUBLISHING.COM

Copyright © 2009 by Shannon R. Bellamy

ISBN 0-7414-5663-X

Cover design by:	Monster Graphic Design
	Chase Design and Print
Author photos:	Shannon Bellamy Enterprises
	Stephen Hudgins Photography
	Digital Grey Photography
Edited by	Joel B. Walker

www.shannonbellamy.com

Published by:

1094 New DeHaven Street, Suite 100
West Conshohocken, PA 19428-2713
Info@buybooksontheweb.com
www.buybooksontheweb.com
Toll-free (877) BUY BOOK
Local Phone (610) 941-9999
Fax (610) 941-9959

Printed in the United States of America

Published October 2009

ACKNOWLEDGMENTS

This book is dedicated to my daughters' thank you for your patience during my all-night, all-day book writing sessions. And to all women; most particularly to young ladies who find themselves struggling with their self image while lost in an ocean of betrayal and a mountain of deception, they hopelessly search to find their emotional and spiritual anchor. My prayer is that God will use me to empower others by sharing my own trials and tribulations as I have battled courageously to win back my soul and self respect after being betrayed by my Spiritual Counselor & Pastor.

INTRODUCTION

Based on a true story

A married Pastor of a Mega Church is exposed for manipulating one of his many counselees into an inappropriately intimate relationship. Read how he plotted methodically to gain her trust while she was at the lowest point in her life, and how she was convinced by her Pastor and Counselor to have an abortion, divorce her husband, and get thousands of dollars in cosmetic surgery, the latter resulting in her near death experience.

CONTENTS

CONTENTS

CONTENTS

Preface

Just as the bible reminds us to be mindful of false prophets; we should also be wary of abusers, disguised as Spiritual Counselors, with the sole mission of luring women into their web of deception as they seek to prey upon our vulnerability, only to have us exiled when they are done with us, leaving us to pick up the pieces all alone...how indicative of a "Pimp".

The Million Dollar Question...

Do I still love him? Yes I do, the way God intended me to, not the way I once did. Loving someone is real, no matter how it happens. I struggled with being in love with my Pastor who was also my Counselor, a man that I was manipulated into having a relationship with, and a church I trusted my life and spiritual well-being. I've come to the conclusion that what has taken place is wrong and goes against everything I have ever been taught growing up and most of all hurts the heart of God! I am now working through the hurt, pain, deception, and betrayal that ripped me to my core, yet I believe God for full restoration, forgiveness, and CHANGE for everyone involved. I forgive him and most importantly I have forgiven myself.

You might have Won the Battle
but you haven't Won the War

~ *Who is Shannon Bellamy* ~

Who am I?

It was not until today, October 18, 2002 at 10:45 am before I could thoroughly answer that question. At that point the mystery unfolded.

Who am I? I am an African American woman with strong features much like my mother's; I look like her the most out of my six siblings. I also have her tiny ankles, and pear shaped figure. I have what I now know to be my daddy's nose. I have inherited his flamboyant, suave, debonair, flashy style and ways.

When I was a little girl, I wanted desperately to be lighted-skinned like my younger sister, and to be short like my older sister. I grew up thinking I was black, ugly, and skinny with no shape and long legs.

Who am I? Today I can tell you, it took writing this essay on "I'm Just Me" for me to find out just who I am, where I came from, and why I am the way that I am.

My father, Robert Bellamy, an African American man, had been a mystery to me. Before today, I only knew that I had a father who had died in a tragic accident when I was a baby. I cannot remember ever seeing his face. Until today, my mother has never told me anything about my daddy. I had a stepfather growing up, however my desire to know who my real father was began to overwhelm me. Sitting here typing my paper, the word daddy sounds so strange to me, I couldn't really identify with it because I didn't really know what it was to have one.

When I called my mother this morning; I said to her, "Can you give me some information about my father"? This was a question I had wanted to ask her for over twenty-five years. First, she asked me why I wanted to know, I told her it was for my paper. To my surprise without hesitating, she said in a soft, slightly startled, yet professional voice, "Robert", he was very flamboyant, flashy, debonair and suave. It all started to make sense to me now.

My curiosity had gotten the best of me; my mind started racing with questions that I always wanted to ask but was afraid to. I felt like an excited first time reporter who just received their first big story to cover. I asked her, so when & where did you meet him. She replied I met him on my 21st Birthday, I was with my girlfriend at a nightclub, he walked in with a sharp white suit on; a real Dapper Don he was. He looked over my shoulder with his sunglasses on. He was a real handsome guy, she replied. The questions kept coming, "were you and my father a couple when he died", she said "no, we were friends." "Were you in love with him", she replied "no, we were just really good friends"; "so, who named me and where did my name come from, she replied I named you. I got your name from a commercial for a Disney telephone, being slightly puzzled I said to her, what, they were selling a Shannon telephone. She said no the little girl in the commercial answered the telephone and said, "Hello my name is Shannon". "I liked the name Shannon, which is how you got your name. Next, I asked her, how my father died, and how old was I when it happened. She replied he was killed in July or August of 1970, in a motorcycle accident in Newark; you were about three months old. He was around 24 or 25 years old at the time. "Did he have nice teeth", she replied, "yes he did, and he was a good-looking suave country boy from the Carolina's."

It all started to make sense to me, why I like the things I like. I like myself a man with nice teeth, who is suave, and debonair, however, I do not like a flamboyant man. I like a strong yet meek and humble man.

I am the flamboyant one.

Who am I? I am my father's child.

Who am I? All of my life, I never felt like I fit in. Nowhere did I feel I was accepted. I was made fun of by my classmates and so-called friends. My siblings and I were estranged. My older sister and brother were very close; my mother had married and divorced their father. My younger sister and two brothers were close; my mother also had married and divorced their father. Then there I was whose parents were never married, they were not even a couple, actually my parents were really nothing more than friends. I always felt left out and not accepted, I was the black sheep of the family.

My grandmother passed away on May 24 this year, we call her Nana, and she is my Queen. She took me and raised me for most of my childhood. I enjoyed living with her and my grandfather. My grandfather was from Louisiana, he stood at 6 foot 7, and we called him Big Daddy or BaDa. I would sit and watch my grandmother; she was a fierce Diva, she wore beautiful elegant gowns and made a stunning entrance wherever she went, back then it was called being sophisticated. My grandmother taught me how to be Diva and introduced me to eloquent dining. My Nana treated me as if I was her baby. Even in my grandmother's latter years, she would always remember to call me on my birthday. She would also send me a birthday card and write in it; today is the day God blessed BaDa and I with you. However, this year the call never came in and my birthday card never made it to me. I did not know that May 7, 2002 would be the last time I would hear her voice. Nana was rushed to the hospital on May 9, 2002 and passed away on May 24, 2002. She died from a short battle with lung cancer.

Happy memories of my childhood come from being with my grandparents. I can remember going to Charlie Brown's with my grandparents when they had the all-you-can-eat shrimp bar. We would dine sufficiently. It was truly a treat. When my Nana would cook at home, to me she was the world's greatest chef. She introduced me to asparagus and sirloin steak; this was classy and expensive stuff back then. I would watch her in the kitchen and ask questions as she cooked. She always took the time to explain to me what she was doing. She taught me to cook, sew, care for my home, and family, and what is was to be a strong woman. My grandmother was and is a Phenomenal Woman.

Who am I? I am my grandmother's child.

Who am I? Someone who misses her Nana.

When I was thirteen my grandparents moved to Louisiana, my mother would not let me move with them. I was forced to stay in East Orange, a place I hated. This place was my modern day hell. I could not go to school for fear of being jumped by a group of girls in the hallway or after school. I was bullied and picked on everyday for no reason at all. . I quit school in the ninth grade. I can remember working my first summer job and earning about $150.00, the school bully waited for me at the check-cashing place to take my paycheck from me. I felt like I was in the wilderness, no one to rescue me.

Who am I? I am a Child of God.

I can remember getting pregnant at the age of fifteen. My oldest brother and I were fighting and he pushed me into a wall. I said to him; stop you're going to hurt my stomach. He immediately ran and told my mother that he thought I was pregnant. Not at all nurturing she said to me, "Oh, so you're pregnant, you're not having an abortion. At that point, all I could do is pray. I did not want a baby I was a baby myself. I can remember going to the clinic for my examination to find out how far along I was.

Sitting in the waiting room, all alone, I might add I prayed as if I never prayed before. I told God that I did not want to have a baby. I know God heard my prayers.

Who am I? I am saved by God's Grace.

Without warning, while sitting in the waiting room I started hemorrhaging. It was as if someone had just turned the faucet on. I was in no pain. Because I was a minor, I needed a parent or guardian to sign for treatment. The clinic gave me a sheet to wrap around myself and told me I needed to go get my parents. My stepfather lived down the street from the clinic at the time. I walked down East Harrison Street in East Orange with a sheet wrapped around me with blood rushing out of me. My stepfather called the ambulance and rushed me to the hospital. Upon my arrival at the hospital, I was informed that I had miscarried. I can remember crying, not because I was in pain, but because God heard my prayers. I do not remember how they found out, but my godparents came to see me in the hospital. My own mother never came to see about me.

Who am I? I am now A woman.

At the age of fifteen, because of the problems and sexual abuse at home, I left and went to Paterson. I met my son's father, who is 17 years older than I am. I got a fake id to make me 18 years old. I worked two to three jobs at a time to earn a living. I am no stranger to hard work. We lived together for 6 years. He had been the lesser of the two evils; he was a way out of my living hell. The relationship between him and I was horrible. He tried to be my father and my man. He wanted to punish me as if I was his child and love me as if I was his wife. It did not work. He was trying to raise me to be the woman he wanted me to be. Nevertheless, something inside of me would not let that happen.

Who am I? I am a survivor.

At the age of 19, I had my son; at the age of 21 I prayed and asked God for a way out of this nightmare. Tired of the physical, mental & emotional abuse, I took the clothes on my back, my baby and his diaper bag, and I left my son's father. I do not regret the relationship, it taught me to how to stand on my own two feet, be a woman at a young age and to survive. I also do not regret leaving him. I walked away and never looked back. My baby and I started what was the first day of the rest of our life. I knew then that I wanted more out of life then what I he had to offer. I could not subject myself to his abuse any longer. I started blooming like a Stargazer Lily on a perfect summer day.

Who am I? I am Determined.

In December 1990, I met a young man named Ronnie Mobley, who was from Teaneck. Ronnie and I worked at Garden State Plaza in Paramus. One day over lunch, we were talking and I told Ronnie about my living situation in Paterson. Ronnie told me his mom was renting out her basement. It was fully furnished, I moved to Teaneck in January 1991; my son was 1 ½ years old. God answered my prayers. When my baby and I moved to Teaneck, life was beautiful. Ronnie's parents took us in and made my baby and me a part of their family, 18 years later Ronnie and I are still friends, no we are "family".

Who am I? A leader and determined to Succeed.

I let the system work for me. I got on welfare, put my baby in daycare and enrolled in Business Training Institute, without having a high school diploma; I graduated at the top of my class. Business Training Institute gave me the skills to do what I do today. Twelve years later I am a seasoned professional executive administrative assistant in a large company.

Who am I? I am about to realize "just how beautiful I am."

Today I know I am an African American Woman who lives for Jesus Christ; I am Shannon Renee Robinson, a 32-year-old divorcee, and single mother of four. I am a part-time college student studying Culinary Art & Restaurant Management, I have a dream to fulfill, a restaurant to open, "A Taste of a Nation". I am a full-time professional executive administrative assistant. I am my father and grandmother's child, someone who misses her Nana, and a child of Child, who was saved by God's grace. I am a survivor, who is determined to be a leader and succeed. I know that I am beautiful; I was spoiled rotten, and then was a baby boomer that was selfish and had to lose it all because I needed to learn a lesson. I was looking for love in all the wrong places, and then loved by God.

1

A World Wind Romance

*I*t was December 1, 2003, I've been divorced for 2 ½ years now and I was ready for love again…

I met a man online at a popular website called Blackpeoplemeet. This young man was an Army reservist and had a civilian job on the army base as a Bio-med technician. We talked on the phone about seven to eight times a day. I enjoyed talking to him, I was such a chatterbox, but he never seemed to mind, he would just listen very attentively. On December 20th, he decided to ask me to join him for dinner on Christmas Day with his family. Of course, I was elated, what a nice offer I thought to myself. My children were going to be with their father on Christmas day since I was going to have them with me Christmas Eve. I accepted his invitation. A few days before Christmas he asked if we could meet ahead of time so it wouldn't be obvious that this was our first physical meeting.

On December 22nd, we met at a half waypoint on the NJ Turnpike. We went to a restaurant of my choosing. Dinner and conversation was all good, I thought to myself he looked just as cute in person as he did in his online pictures. He was brown-skinned; 6'2, medium build, wore cute glasses and spoke quite eloquently. After dinner we went our separate ways in preparation for our Christmas date. The next day was my middle daughter's birthday, we celebrated, just me and my four children. On Christmas Eve I stayed up wrapping presents for the kids. It has been a tradition that Santa comes Christmas Eve in the middle of the night; we'd leave fresh baked cookies and milk for Santa. No presents appear under the tree until Santa came. Here they go, 6 o'clock in the morning and my children are screaming' in my ear.

"Mommy wake up"

"Wake up, Santa came"

"Santa came."

So I get up and get the video camera to videotape the kids on Christmas morning opening their gifts. After breakfast and baths everyone is dressed and settled, it's time to drop the kids off at their dad's house. My date arrives and we travel to Philadelphia to his family's house. The ride to Philadelphia was uneventful and we were able to have some great conversation on the ride down. Once there he introduced me to his family, we had a great time; the food was good too. I am naturally picky, and being a Chef I have acquired a certain pallet, so everyone cannot cook for me. I had on a cute Karl Kani denim pants and jacket combination, and had been feeling really cute, but after dinner uh, I felt stuffed. I remember having to open up the button on my jeans. Thank God I don't have to drive, because I got the "itis'.

After dinner I sat there patiently while he conversed with his family. Finally it was time to go, but before we headed back to North Jersey, he took me on a scenic tour of Philadelphia. He showed me the famous Clothespin, Boathouse Row, the Art Museum, and the beautiful statues in Fairmount Park. What a romantic evening I thought…Nice…he was such a gentleman, and oh so romantic… all the things I'd been looking for in a man.

We arrived back at my place around 2 a.m., I extended the offer for him to stay in one of the extra bedrooms since the kids were gone for the evening, and he accepted. We spent much of the next day watching movies, laughing and talking. Well it was time for me to get it cracking; I had a wedding to cater, and I was pleased that he offered to stay and help me with the catering job. He diced and sliced as I prepared the food for a 150 person gala. He would take the time to come and give me sweet kisses on my neck while I cooked. I was cool as a cucumber but my insides were churning, I thought to myself, Whaaaat, no way….he is Mr. Perfect….

It's that time; time to get this show on the road. We go to the catering hall with all the food and supplies, and I am ready for a Shannon Bellamy Custom-Made Catering production. While I was in the kitchen plating my "Signature Salad" he walks pass me while on the phone, and I overheard him telling his friend, "She's the one." I laugh, "Stop playing on the phone, no one is on it." He laughs and gives me the phone. I'm thinking I'll humor him and say hello, but to my surprise I hear hello on the other end. I introduced myself, and then got back to the business of plating the salads. The wedding and reception went off without a hitch. Everything was perfect. I was running around doing this and that but was in total control of the evening, everything was beautiful. I worked really hard on it and I was really happy with the successful outcome. At the end of the night he helped me clean up, gather my things and we went back to my house.

He was having such a good time that he didn't want to go home. The next day he went to work then came right back to my house. He helped me cook and we sat around watching movies. He started to open up some more and the conversation between us was engaging, the compatibility was evident too, he was easy going and I liked that. Well, now my children are home, and its New Years Eve, just as the ball dropped….

…..he dropped….

….down on his knees and asked me to marry him.

…..Yes you heard it right, and he asked me to marry him.

Just after knowing him 30 days…that is a record even for me! Of course I said yes, I had been on a cloud for the last 30 days. I felt like I deserved to be happy, after all I'd been single for 2 ½ years now. Over the next couple of weeks he was perfect, while I was in culinary school he would take my son to football practice or pick him up from school.

……He cooked and even washed my clothes.

Oh wait!

He washed that pile of clothes in the bottom of the Hamper that…Only 'You' Wash!

Can't you just clutch your pearls!

Huh, he had the nerve to tell me that he washed the clothes and if anything was a "bit dirtier" than he thought…

…he just scrubbed it out!

I tell you "I Clutched My Pearls"…that is funny, Oh My God I said, I am definitely going to marry him now, he will not be talking about me. You know how it is…that was funny. I called my girlfriends screaming and laughing on the phone about him doing my "personal" laundry.

About a week later we began searching around for catering halls. We chose a date of October 2004. I felt like that would be good, although we got engaged rather quickly I knew that we would have 10 months to get to know each other. Well to my surprise a week later he tells me there is a possibility he would soon have to go overseas for 18 months. I told him no problem we can just wait to get married when he returns from Germany. He insisted that he wanted to be married before he left; he said that if he didn't go we would just have our wedding ceremony as planned with our family and friends in October. Reluctantly, I said okay. When he, my girlfriend and I went to get the marriage license; he was acting a bit anxious and jittery. When I asked him what was wrong, he said nothing. He said he just wanted to be my husband and provide for our children. So off I go to David's Bridal to look for a wedding dress and shoes. He was easy; he wore his "dress greens" for the Army.

The night before the wedding we stayed up late cooking together making appetizers and such for our intimate nuptials.

Just five weeks after our first date we were married, on was January 18, 2004

Our children were not present. His 4-year-old daughter was with her mother, and my children were with their father.

It was a beautiful winter afternoon, a bit cloudy but it was nice outside. My brother, who is an ordained minister married us; our guests included my mother and our closest friends. We were married at my home. After the ceremony we went outside to take some pictures. It started to snow, it was the most beautiful sight; the silhouette of snow in the pictures looked so pretty. My husband's best man was a co-worker who was also a reservist. The couple I had catered the wedding for, Mr. & Mrs. Henry and Vanessa Drummond was also there. Vanessa's husband was honored to fill in for my deceased father, and walked me down the aisle. It was so beautiful. Later that night my now husband told me it was love at first sight for him. I couldn't believe this was happening to me.

I felt like Cinderella at the ball, midnight came too soon…we were married on Sunday, and five days later he was deployed to Germany.

Was the marriage a scam? Did he marry me so quickly for a reason? Hmmm

Now what? My girlfriends cried with me. I was so devastated. I picked up the pieces yet again and continued with my life. I was in Culinary School and I was graduating in May, no matter what was going on in my personal life I had to finish school. It has always been my desire to open a Restaurant & Supper Club.

Graduation was three months away and the unemployment and severance that I was living on had depleted. My new husband wasn't sending money home at the time. I was living off of $800.00 a month in child support and the help of my girlfriend Vanessa. Vanessa would come over and ask me to do her hair, she would "conveniently" leave $100 each time for me doing her hair. I never charged her, and I would gladly do her hair for free but she made sure I had enough money for gas and incidentals so that I could finish school. I never wanted to borrow any money from anyone because I didn't know when I could repay it.

It was graduation time, it was so emotional. My mother and my children were there, I cried when I walked into the auditorium. The emotion hit me like a brick. It was the first time I had ever had on a cap and gown and graduated. I had received my GED just two years prior, this was a major accomplishment for me and I did it in spite of all the drama surrounding my life and obstacles in the way.

2

A Fresh Start for My Family

*I*t was now October 2004; I was ready for a fresh start. After a three-year caustic divorce and custody battle, where I'd lost custody of my two youngest daughters when they were four and five years old, I was ready to make the necessary adjustments in my life for my family. I needed to be in a place where I did not have a constant reminder of my failed marriage or my failure to retain custody of my daughters. I fought a long and agonizing custody battle with my ex-husband over our daughters. He had custody of our daughters for three years, and I continued the court battle until one day my Aunt Nancy said to me…

"You are not going to die! He is their father and has every right to raise them as you do."

At that point I stopped fighting and decided to pick up the pieces of my life and start to live life and figure out a way to bring a certain quality of life to my four children in spite of our situation. After I graduated culinary school I was at a crossroad, I wasn't sure about my direction. Then I met a man who knew me when I was a child, he sat me down and told me that I should go into Real Estate. I did not like the thought of being a salesperson, even though I am a people person and have the gift of gab. I never did. I always ran away from commission jobs, huh, I need my money every other Friday without fail.

After a couple of hours he convinced me how free and financially well off my life would be if I sold real estate. He was making a killing back then; it was the beginning of the big real estate boom. He sat there and convinced me to go to Real Estate School. I thought what the heck; at the very least I would have something else to add to my repertoire, so I went to a real estate school in North Jersey.

Then I thought since I was about to go to real estate school it was time for relocation. I was looking for a new place to call home when I felt led to go to Willingboro, NJ. I didn't know anything about the area, but my cousin lives in Burlington and I thought that Willingboro/Burlington was a great area. I drove two hours down the Turnpike with my children just to get their local paper. I found an ad for a house in the newspaper and it asked to contact the landlord's realtor. I met with the realtor and we saw the house, the house was perfect; well landscaped, in-ground swimming pool, four bedrooms, living room, dining room, office, entertainment room and the neighborhood was absolutely beautiful. I told the realtor that I was in the process of getting my real estate license. She told me that I should consider joining her office. When we got back to the office to complete paperwork for the house, she introduced me to her real estate broker. He was a sharp, tall, distinguished man in his late 40's. He was a smooth one. After I met with him she sat me down with her office manager. Now that was a classy dame! I had never seen such a beautiful and classy woman with such a killer walk. I thought to myself I had to try and imitate that walk! The meeting went well and I went back home to consider my options for which real estate office I would work for, I had interviewed with a couple of offices near my current home but they just didn't feel right.

I had a lot on my mind and a lot of decisions to make.

I was trying to come to terms with yet another failed attempt at a marriage, my new marriage seemingly being a scam, and me yet again being single.

Three weeks later on October 24, 2004, I successfully passed the New Jersey Real Estate Exam. This was the new beginning I was searching for...I was so excited. I called my friend in California and told him that I passed the State exam; it was such a good feeling.

I felt like I was on top of the world.

In late November I went back down to Willingboro and settled on a house to rent. While I was waiting for the owners to relocate to Florida, I decided to look at more real estate offices in the area. I went to one office and I felt so out of place; nope it's not for me I thought. Then I went to another and I wasn't "feeling" that office either. I settled on the office that my realtor was with. After successfully finding a house to rent, I began packing and preparing to move my children into our new home. Five months later, my family and I are still living out of boxes waiting for the owners to relocate. Every month it's a different story. Apparently, that was not the house for me and God blocked it. In April 2005, the house I was waiting to rent fell through and I was back at the drawing board. I had been driving 1 ½ hours each way six days a week to South Jersey to sell real estate. I was getting my hustle on. I didn't miss not one training class I was soaking up everything my broker was teaching. Other real estate agents felt "some kind of way" because I immediately became the "favorite" of the Broker and Office Manager's.

They just enjoyed my vigor and thirst for life. I'd been through enough, and just wanted to be happy and secure.

I was doing so well in real estate that I bought myself a Mercedes Benz for my birthday. I had been watching the lot at Jonathan Motor Cars in Edgewater Park, NJ…
It was time! I walked in the showroom with $10,000.00 in my hand and said to the salesman,

"Clean her up," I'll be back after lunch for… Miss 'Black on Black Mercedes Benz CLK 320'.

Despite the sweet new wheels, I began to get frustrated with the new house search. My co-worker Tanya suggested Sicklerville, NJ. Since I was now an official realtor, it would be easy for me to do my own search in the system. She said Sicklerville was a growing community and a nice place to raise children. I was "rocking and rolling" selling real estate. Money was coming and coming faster than I could put it in my pocket.

I looked and found a home to rent that was newly constructed. My co-worker Bobby drove me to Sicklerville since I was unfamiliar with the area. When we went to look at the house I thought wow it's perfect. It's brand new and more than enough for my children and I. Strangely enough I got a sign told me that this was it! What was the sign you ask? The sign was my stomach; it started aching and I had to use the bathroom - bad. Like most people I am particular about using the bathroom anywhere other than home. However, this time I couldn't wait; I took it as a sign that I was home. I contacted the other agent, did the paperwork and May 15th here we come, our new life and fresh start.

Freedom, Peace & Serenity!

I knew that my visitations every other weekend with my daughters would be a sacrificial one because I had a 2 ½ hour ride each way, however, I was so ready for this much needed change and fresh start to this brand new home in a beautiful neighborhood with lots of green grass.

While we were waiting for the movers to come with the furniture, I noticed my children rolling around on the grass in the front yard. This was a very happy moment for me. I was happy that my children were happy. They ran through the house screaming thank you mommy, thank you!

I went in a corner all to myself and cried.

My children were happy.

As a parent that is all we want for our children.

As the new neighbors drove by they stopped and welcomed us to the neighborhood, and all afternoon people were saying hello and welcoming us. I must admit it felt tremendous!

Ut oh!

By early June we were all unpacked and settled in. It was at this point that the excitement started to wear off, and I started to unravel. The kids were all gone for the weekend, and I became home sick. I really missed my friends back up

North, so I got dressed and started up Route 295. I got about 45 minutes up the highway and said to myself, "what are you doing?!" This is your home now. So I turned around and started heading back. I then began to reason that I was lonely, and just wanted to hang out in So-Ho in NYC with my girlfriends, so I turned around again and started driving back up North. Then I thought I need to...

"Stop running"

"Go back to my new home and...."

"Embrace the change."

I stopped on my way home to pick up dinner. Once home, I proceeded straight to a bubble bath, and then rocked myself new sleep – in my new home.

3

My place of Refuge….or so I thought

The next morning the neighbor who lives across the street came over to introduce himself. He told me he is a married man with two children and the Minister of Music at his church and invited me to attend. The next morning he called me at 6:00 a.m. to wake me so that I could follow him to the church since I didn't know my way. The senior pastor preached his name was….Dum Dum Dum Dummm Pastor Keith W. Reed Sr. he was born and raised in Philadelphia, Pennsylvania. He was in his late 40's but could pass for 20 years old all day long! He stood around 5'8, roughly 185lbs, and stayed in LA Fitness…he kept a Steve Harvey Suit on….Sunday's he would come in laced up, glisten' lookin' like "new money" with a fresh hair cut and a tight goatee, his voice….Barry White with just enough Baby Face on it (he was smooth), he would "drop it like it's hot" on the pulpit mocking the new dances in his introduction to the congregation; he kept the women in the congregation lusting after him….. only "Gators" will do for him (he has them in every color), his "jew'ells" he has a 2" Platinum Bible on his right hand ring finger and a diamond wedding band big enough to make any "woman" jealous. He would preach and would have you coming out your seat…whatever he was selling you were buying – No questions asked! Not to mention his flashy vehicles to include his silver BMW 745iL, truck, Harley Davidson Motorcycles and a host of toy cars in his driveway in his Woodbury, NJ mansion. He is now "Bishop" Reed, he is over a host of churches including one in Maryland. I tell you, I felt it was the biggest mock of the "Bishop" order when he became Bishop. There were so many women coming forward alleging that they were involved with him romantically. Pastor Caines told me that he had to write a letter to the head of the Bishop's organization to smooth things over so that they would allow Pastor Reed to become Bishop. One of women Bishop Reed was allegedly having an affair with was asked to leave and sent to another Philadelphia Mega church. I really thought that being a "Bishop" was something great and that the person taking this position would have had to demonstrate certain leadership capabilities and disciplines in their personal lives before they would be bestowed such a position. I guess that is not always the case. This Sunday his sermon was on the "Power of the Hand vs. the Glove." It was so awesome, and so powerful, that I joined the church that day. My spirit was so stirred up that as soon as I heard the altar call I forgot all about the 3,000 plus worshippers in the building and walked straight down the aisle without fear.

Because I was a visitor of the Minister of Music, I was seated in the fifth row. I returned on Tuesday for Bible Study and the following Sunday. I was hungry for the Word of God. The very next week I went and sat in the same row, although it was a different preacher teaching this day. I thought "Oh my God", another amazing sermon! This time the topic was about "Struggles"; he referenced his body by stretching out his arms and swaying from right to left, while saying he struggles just like people in the pews do. I was so moved by his sermon that I walked up to him and told him how moving it was for me. I called him Pastor Reed, he said I am not Pastor Reed baby; Dum Dum Dum Dummm "I am Pastor Caines." I was like wow....what a sermon Pastor Caines. Huh, this Bermuda born, Internationally known Pastor had a very distinguished look, at 52 years old standing at 6'2 he keeps that "Just for Men" box handy...Jet Black! He has a Caribbean peanut butter skin complexion and a voice.....he says it, it sounds mmm mmm good.....he speaks so eloquently and proper, every word is "pronounced." He has a British accent and wears glasses and keeps his head nicely waved up. Sexy is his past and definitely his present. He was best known for being "Mr. Quiet Storm" in Bermuda; he was a Radio Disc Jockey. He was a real "ladies man" in his day! When he walks across the stage (pulpit) it looks likes he is gliding with that bowlegged stroll of his. This Sunday he thanked me for the compliment and welcomed me to the church; I walked to the foyer and waited for my neighbor so I could follow him back home.

The next Sunday I went again, this time I took my four children. At that time my son was 15, and my daughters were 11, 8 and 7. We sat in same row that I had in the previous two weeks. About ten minutes after my children and I sat down here comes an usher. She was curt; she told my oldest daughter that we had to move. I stood up and politely whispered excuse me, she said we couldn't sit there, that those seats were for special guests. I explained to her that I had been sitting there for the past two weeks; she said she didn't care and told me I had to move. I felt this was an unnecessary disruption of the service simply because she wanted to make it known that she was "in-charge". I was so angry I told my children not to move and went to her and asked if I could speak to her outside. When we got into the hall I told her she better not ever disrespect me again in that tone. During the conversation the Head of Security walked up and introduced himself. He said, "I am Toney are you okay?" I began to explain what had happened and he allowed me and my children to remain where we were and directed the usher to go back inside. He told me if I ever had any trouble to come and see him. I asked him who was in charge of the Ushers; and he told me Pastor Caines was in charge of the Usher's Ministry.

After service was over I approached Pastor Caines, I went up to him and realized he was the same Pastor who preached the previous week. When I began to tell him about the Usher's behavior, he said to me that I was "out of order." When I said, "I beg your pardon".

He said, "I've seen your kind before,

It's not all about you."

I was numb at that point and couldn't believe what I was hearing. I remember thinking to myself, so this is how a Mega church is run? He told me to call him on Tuesday to discuss the matter further.

Previously I had met Pastor Darryl Robinson, he was the Pastor of Preservation, our introduction was brief and I just told him that my name was previously Robinson. When Tuesday came I contacted Pastor Robinson to tell him what Pastor Caines had said and to inquire if that was procedure. Pastor Robinson referred me right back to Pastor Caines.

When Pastor Caines answered the phone, he said to me, "I've seen your type before"; I didn't know what that statement meant. I am from the New York tri-state area and I am pretty much like most of the progressive women in the North. He proceeded to tell me that I was star struck, (I know he meant I was acting like a high maintenance Diva); I said to him it's not my fault that people sometimes act like they recognize me when they see me, people mistake me for Patti Labelle, Sheryl Lee Ralph and Anna Maria Horsford all the time. He said that he could "help me" and invited me in for a counseling session. He turned the conversation around and was now attempting to have a more therapeutic approach. After our conversation I set up an appointment with his secretary to meet with him for counseling.

4

My Spiritual Accountability

O nce I arrived he asked me all about my past and my ex-husbands. He spent time getting to know all about me; and during his inquiries about my strengths, weaknesses, struggles, fears, accomplishments, goals and other very personal and sensitive information, he suggested that I be very explicit. Over time I told him everything, about the sexual abuse I endured as a child, being repeatedly raped for two years from the age of eleven by my mother's boyfriend and then just to leave home at the age of 15 to be physically abused by my son's father for over six years; my son's father was 19 years older than me, he treated me like I was his wife but punished me like I was his child. Pastor Caines and I began discussing my dating habits and during our discussions I told him that I was on Blackpeoplemeet, a popular dating website. He then told me to give him my username and password. This is when the control started.

That was the dating website I had been using since 2002. He was uncompromising about me dating online and proceeded to delete my profile right in front of me. When I explained to him that I'd rather date online because the likelihood of the men being in other relationships are slim, he said "absolutely not, only street women and whores are on dating websites." I said to him the site is full of single professional people. It has been my observations that because men are "ocular" (Pastor Caines' word) when you meet them in public, and they like what they see, it is more likely you will meet someone who is already involved with someone else. I told him that I don't date married men or want to date someone else's man!

"He knew what was best for me; he said, "I know you almost better than you know yourself."

Even after our first meeting, he said this. He knew my type because "he's seen my type before". He was the expert in "my" type, whatever that meant...only he knew! He was good; he got right into my head. Pastor Caines has a Doctorate of Divinity hanging proudly on his wall in his office. Of the five pastors at Bishop Keith W. Reed Sr.'s church (aka Sharon Baptist Church at 3955 Conshohocken Avenue in Philadelphia, Pennsylvania) he was the one to counsel most of the members even though he only had an "honorary" Doctorate of Divinity, and no formal training as a counselor. Come to find out he didn't even have an Associate's Degree.

I knew something wasn't right when one Sunday while Pastor Reed was preaching, he said that the Pastors at Sharon Baptist Church were "known" for being the "Pistol Packin' Preachers", I wondered, why they would be carrying pistols, are these men really preachers or are they "Pimpin from the Pulpit?"

At least every three to four weeks I was scheduled to see Pastor Caines for counseling. This went on indefinitely, and now that he was my counselor, I was forbidden to see any other Pastor in the church.

In addition to our office time we would talk on the phone approximately 8 to 10 times a day. Before I realized it, he had become a part of my day-to-day life. The more he counseled, the more I believed and trusted his every word.

5

"A Real Wolf in Sheep's Clothing"

fter about three weeks of attending the church, I became aware that the youth ministry was planning a skating trip. I thought it would be nice for my children to participate and get to know some of the other youth in the church. I couldn't believe what happened next. Here is the actual email I sent to Pastor Caines that next day:

Sunday, August 14, 2005 2:37 PM
From:
"Shannon R. Bellamy"
To:
"K.Glenn Caines"

Hi Pastor Caines,

I didn't want too much time to pass by and not be able to fully recall what happened. On Friday night I took my son and daughter to the skating night in Camden and an "Indecent Proposal" took place.

When I arrived I saw Pastor Darryl Robinson, he said to me how are you, good? I said no I am great! He stated he was glad I made it out, we walked over to a sitting area where you put your skates on and he asked me what the perfume I was wearing was. I told him it was Channel Coco Mademoiselle. He said this will be the only conversation we will have tonight, because he needed to stay away from me. He said perfume smells differently on different people and he said mmmmm. Then he said he had 5 "No's" in him. I didn't understand what that meant so I asked him to clarify, he said he will say "No" 5 times before he gives in....I laughed....I didn't think he was serious...My first thought was this is the "Pastor" he can't be coming onto me. He started laughing and said, yeah, I have some stuff with me (meaning him). He said he didn't get all his "freak out". He asked me

47

how adventurous was I? I said I'm quite adventurous. I didn't know at the time what he was talking about; I thought he was talking about skating and being adventurous on the floor. He said huh,

I want to just take you out back and "eat you out until you cum and you suck me off until I cum".

He asked me to meet him outback at 1 o'clock a.m. I was shocked that he said that to me. I must have showed amazement on my face because he asked me "What you don't do that?" I told him "No"! No I don't. Pastor, you know how uncomfortable I feel about that display of sex. I told him that I was in counsel with you, he laughed and said aight' I am not going to tempt you. But it didn't stop there, although I thought it was inappropriate I did not know how to respond; even though I was somewhat offended I didn't want to cause a sense and offend anyone, I did tell him that I was in counsel with you and that had he made the request two weeks ago perhaps I would have felt different about his proposition. He said, oh, so I am two weeks late, I said yes, two weeks and Pastor C's counsel late.

He said, "You mean to tell me you are telling me No?"

I said yes I am telling you No!

I asked him; what, are trying to send me to "Hell" with big gasoline bloomers on? He laughed. He went off and skated, then every time he or I stopped on the less active side of the skating rink, he continued with his questions. At one point he skated up to me and said it is almost one o'clock a.m. and he asked me what do I like and what am I good at. I told him I am new at this walk, don't mess with me. I am good at what I do and it will mess you up! I told him I was a "Boss", back up! Just leave me alone (in a humorous way).

He told me he wanted to know what it tastes like, "yes the pastor"!

Then he said if they turn down the lights again ...... the short conversations took place about three-four times throughout the evening.

He told me he could have had sex with many women in the church, however, he hadn't because he is afraid they would tell.

Then he asked me would "I tell".

The last time I took a break from skating and sat down, somehow we got on the subject of tattoos, he asked me did I have any, I told him I have one on my back, he asked could he see it, then he touched my butt. I said No!

I couldn't believe this was the Pastor!

Then he said he wanted some tongue before I left (meaning he wanted to kiss me). He told me he had a hard on (clearly he did it was visible).

I was confused.

I told him my husband is coming home from overseas soon and if I am going to mess up it will be with him, not you! I told him again, I had been meeting with you, but never spoke about what you and I talk about.

He said to me, you like the fact that you got me all squirming don't you and he laughed.

I didn't respond then he asked me again, "I said it is flattering". I admit, I thought it was somewhat cute and I flirted back a little,

> but then I heard your voice in my head, saying,
> "What are you "Values"
> and if a man_respects you he will not cause you to do
anything ungodly and that is displeasing to God.
> I thought to myself - he does not Respect me, why?
> I thought about "compromising no-more"!

All I could think about was the sessions I had with you and how I obviously I became sickened by his actions. I tried to play it off and not let him see that I was bothered by it. I said, "I am not messing with you!"

At the end of the evening he walked out to my car and saw the "Ms Bellamy" on the back of my car, I told him that I was going to remove it because of the heat I was getting from you about having my name on my car, that is when a silver colored BMW 745LI pulled up - he then said, you better be glad you got your kids tonight, his son's had taken the bus back with the church. I then asked a young man who walked up to him and started talking how do I get home from here and he said ask my father, his father just happened to be the Pastor Reed. I didn't know until that time it was the senior pastor who had pulled up, the pastor walked over to him to say hello; I asked the senior pastor could I follow him out - he said yes - then we left.

The next day, Revelation....purpose driven...Thessalonians Chap. 4 popped up and I was sickened the more I thought about what had happened. I called my best friend and told them. Pastor I struggled with telling you because I did not want my name a part of a scandal or my integrity questioned with this pastor having been here for 10 years on staff and me five weeks, but Pastor Caines you know I have no reason to lie. He was quite aggressive, so much that I felt like he had me pinned up in a corner. I am the aggressor, I don't like aggressive men, you read that in my papers. I just could not believe that he had said those things to me. Also, I

51

started to question myself and cause blame on myself thinking what I could have ever done for him to think he could say the things he said to me.

*He made me feel like a **"Whore"**!*

he invited me behind a roller-skating rink to perform oral sex on me and me him. He spoke of his wife highly - my question is

"Why did he think he could say that to me?"

I have never been indecent or inappropriate with my conduct, clothing or conversation. I thought about the value system you and I had been discussing. I told him that the minister of music and I are neighbors (he didn't know previously) he asked me did he "hit it" I told him "No"; I said he had the opportunity but never did. I told him that we are each other's keepers and our friendship and relationship with God is too important to do something so easy. He said, huh I would have "hit it". I asked the minister of music did he ever have a conversation with him about me, I was just trying to figure out what made the pastor think he could say those vulgar things to me and that it would be okay. He said, "No, I hadn't" he continued by saying, "it does not surprise me that he did that. He told me that I am the fifth or sixth woman who has come to him about indecent conduct and comments made by that very same pastor. When he told me that I knew I had to tell you, perhaps the others were afraid.

It is a good thing we have been in counsel because this situation would have easily caused me to leave the church.

Pastor, please use this information however you deem fit, I trust you, your judgment and counsel.

I take your counsel extremely serious I even gave your number to Jerome, I told him he had to get the okay from you to go out with me. I feel empowered that I can say "No" - No compromising. God Bless...if you would like to speak further please call me or I will just see you Thursday.

After reporting the incident to Pastor Caines, he in turned reported the incident to the Associate Pastor. They then called me and Pastor Robinson in for a meeting. Pastor Robinson was counseled and sat down from his position for a while; however, he was still able to counsel others during that time. His punishment was...he was not able to preach during the second service to get the offering, which is how the Pastors supplement the difference in their salaries; I later learned that information from Pastor Caines.

When I went back to work on Monday I decided to share what happened at the church with my real estate broker, who was also my friend by this time. He was a Deacon at his church and always kept the bible and its principles before me.

When I told him what had happened and how I handled it he said he was proud of me and for that I was happy.

I guess I am still looking for acceptance and for someone to love me and make me feel important.

Later that evening the Minister of Music and his wife came over to my house, we watched a movie and steamed some crabs, it really meant a lot – for them to be supportive of what happened and extend their friendship. He told me that this is not the first he had heard of this. He even told me that he knew of a few women who Pastor Robinson had actually had sex with in his office during a counseling session, that news sickened me and that is why I am happy I reported him.

Things seemed to have quieted down at church and I am on my "grind" selling real estate. During my counseling session with Pastor Caines he asked me how I was doing in real estate. I told him I am doing great; however, I think it's time my commissions were increased. He said that my broker was taking advantage of me. I told him that my broker was paying my bills (with my money) however he has not increased my commission and I have made over $5,000,000.00 in six months for his company.

I am feeling "some type way right now."

I am afraid for some reason to confront my broker. Pastor Caines told me to stop my broker from paying my bills and to gain control of my money.

I gained control of my money from my broker and things were back on track. Pastor Caines was sending me real estate clients. Whenever he was in a counseling session he would bring up my name and let his counselees know that I was a Real Estate Agent. He introduced me to a couple he was doing pre-marital counseling for, because they were looking for a house at the time. After our meeting I did what I do and found them a fabulous house with all the trimmings. The 4-bedroom house complete with a finished basement and theatre room with movie theatre seating. They were extremely happy. At closing I took a picture of them with their new keys and had the photo framed for them. About a week after they closed on their new home I wanted to do something special for my Pastor and my clients he just referred to me. Therefore, I surprised everyone with a magical evening. I had a limousine pick all of us up. It was Pastor Caines, his wife, my clients and I. While we were driving to the restaurant I gave my clients a gift, it was the photograph from their closing blown up and framed. In addition, I gave both them and Pastor Caines a painting called "Born Again". The painting was a statue of a man whose top half was crystallized and whose bottom half was like a layer of brown cooper being peeled off to reflect him becoming a new creature in Christ. The bottom of the painting had the scripture:

"Therefore if anyone is in Christ, he's a new creature; the old things passed away; behold, new things have come". Corinthians 5:17 NAS.

We all went to dinner at the high rated fine dining destination known as Rat's Restaurant at Grounds for Sculpture in Hamilton, NJ. The restaurant sits on 35-acres of land it has life-size sculptures throughout, it's breathtaking. Everyone dined lavishly I spent over $1,000.00 at dinner alone, the wine never stopped coming; we shut the restaurant down.

Pastor Caines was a good counselor and friend by now, he had walked me through so much transition, and had the backbone in my life. He was so invested in my growth and success. I even won Real Estate Agent of the Year in my office and the Circle of Excellence Multi-Million Dollar Club Award in the state of New Jersey. He would always take the time to read Scriptures to me and was very attentive and just listened. I was content in my home and church life. He said he was investing in my future, and that he couldn't wait to see the "New Shannon Bellamy" the Woman of God that I was called to be.

Wow, I was excited now too…

I wanted to see the new me he was talking about!

6

"The Holidays are approaching, Guess who goes to Jail"

J am preparing to do what I do….entertain. I am planning my Holiday Party at my new home. Now, it's a happy time. I love the Holidays and I love to entertain! Cooking and throwing parties is what I do!

On December 11, 2005 I had a big Holiday party with my colleagues and new friends. My Aunt Peggie came and brought "Uncle Charlie", oh my God he was the highlight of the party with his cane, long beard and clothes "coordinated" like "Pop" the "bang, bang, bang man." It was a great party and turnout.

Just when I think things are going great, why is it when I go to meet my ex-husband; to drop off our daughter's to him on Exit 5 of the NJ Turnpike that he has the police waiting there. He had a warrant issued for my arrest for child support. I didn't even know I had a child support obligation to pay him. Our daughters have two of everything, they do not need to pack a bag when they come to Mommy's house, Mommy has everything they need right there for them. He didn't say a word and had the mail sent to my old address in North Jersey and of course child support won't forward mail. The kicker…I just ran out of the house to drop the girls off, so my clothes weren't matching, I had on a coat, hat, slippers, and "my" hair in a ponytail while carrying my Chanel handbag.

To make matters worse, why was I wearing my bright orange … "Madea Goes to Jail - I Ain't Scared of No Po Po" T-shirt! And just so you know this book is full of "real" accounts…….here it is….

Don't laugh "the Diva" was surely looking a hot mess!

My daughters were crying trying to figure out why the police wanted their mommy. Their father played stupid and acted like he didn't know what was going on. He just pulled off with our daughters and left me there. I called my girlfriend and she put her husband on the phone since, he is a detective. The police would not even allow him to find out what was going on.

As soon as my ex-husband drove off with my kids the police officers looked at my t-shirt and commented that they didn't find it humorous. I said, "Like I knew I would be seeing you today." Why did they then put handcuffs on me and take me to the police station.

I am cool at this point, but I am starting to get a bit nervous because, can I say I am in "Kansas". I had my cell phone and I called my girlfriend Lisa from the real estate office to let her know what had happened. I was taken from Westampton to Burlington County; I called Pastor Caines and left him a message. Once at Burlington County the correction officer, who checked me in, was really nasty. She took my purse and dumped it upside down and when she saw my business cards she started mocking and making jokes. Oh, so we have a professional here ladies! The experience was the worst. They made me shower with ice cold water, sprayed me for lice, had me spread eagle and cough, and then when she realized I had a nipple ring she tried to take it out and caused me to bleed.

A lot of correction officer's act inhumane.

They forget that outside of that uniform they are regular civilians and not everyone that comes there is a hardened criminal, no matter what reason a person is incarcerated they deserve to be treated with respect.

They took me to a cell and gave me a boat to sleep on, the boat was a portable plastic bed; it was hard like a toddler's toy. The woman who was in this 4x6 cell I joined was in there for child support as well. She told me she had been there for five days waiting for Cumberland County to come get her. I started to get nervous because my case was out of Bergen County. How long is it going to take for them to come get me I thought? But then I realized it is "Bergen County" they are pretty efficient up there, to a fault! I wouldn't eat anything; the woman said I'd be in trouble with the officers if I didn't eat. I did not care, they were not going to feed me that garbage, I will take my chances. I just laid there and prayed. I knew God was not about to let me stay there any extended time. When the morning came, they came around with some nasty breakfast, nope! I wasn't eating that either. I was numb I didn't want anything but "Out!"

Around 9:00 a.m. I heard someone say "Bellamy get your things" just like in "Madea Goes to Jail" the movie, I got up and hauled *!@# When the guard came to get me I broke down, I started crying and vomiting. I was so upset over this entire ordeal.

When the sheriff officers came to transport me back to Bergen County they said, "The hard part is over." They allowed me to put my civilian clothes back on, what good that freakin' did, I came in wearing my bright orange "Madea Goes to Jail" t-shirt. It was a 2 hour ride to Bergen County. The officer said I am taking the scenic route back and handed me my cell phone. I was able to call my real estate broker, mom, girlfriend Lisa and Pastor Caines. When I arrived in Bergen County I was re-processed, by the time they were done Lisa had picked up my money from my broker and posted the bail, which was the amount of the child support and I was free to go. Oh my God, why did she laugh when she saw the t-shirt and the way I was dressed. She took a picture of me looking straight crazy *(you saw the picture)*. Till this day I never wore that t-shirt again, but I kept it for a souvenir (smile).

The next day I went to work like nothing ever happened, I had real estate deals to make happen and customers to show houses to. Nothing was going to stop my grind! Life is always going to throw you a curve ball, it's up to you whether you hit it or let it hit you! I called my daughters with my high perky voice to put their little souls at rest that their mommy was okay.

Life was back to normal, my normal!

I signed up for classes at church, they have a Biblical Institute within the church; I was working toward my certificate in Christian Leadership. One of the classes I took was called "Marital Issues". Pastor Caines told me that I couldn't go to the singles ministries because I was not officially single therefore the only ministry left was the married ones. This class turned out to be great; I learned a lot about the roles and responsibilities of both a husband and a wife. At first I felt awkward in the class then I saw there were other women there whose husbands didn't even come to church. I wanted to make sure that when my husband came home from the military that if in fact our marriage was not a scam that I would give it the best possible chance at survival. After two failed marriages I was determined to make this one work in spite of how it began.

The class was taught by Pastor Peterson and his wife. This couple was my favorite at church; this was the only Pastor who had not allowed infidelity to creep into their marriage. All the rest had rumors of infidelity surrounding their marriages by the dozens. Pastor Peterson spoke so highly of his wife and quite openly expressed all the things he would do to make her feel special; including the "us" time he would set aside to be with her, minus the kids. He even bragged about going shopping for his wife and picking out her clothes and shoes. I felt inspired and encouraged by their relationship. They both were very honest about their lives together, including how they endured, and finally overcame poverty, and many of the other struggles that life can present. His wife, being a very intelligent woman in her own right, eloquently added balance to her husband's teaching ministry.

Pastor Peterson reminded me of my son's father. They actually looked like they could be brothers, and when my son saw him for the first time he said, "Mom, wow he looks just like my dad. Every time I saw Pastor Peterson and his wife it made me feel proud, proud that there are still some marriages out there that are willing to fight it out to the end to keep their marriage sacred. He even spoke about the drug abuse, having unreliable transportation and his dedication to the church while having his family in tow.

After each counseling session with Pastor Caines he would always remind me to make another appointment with his secretary. In October 2005, my husband finally came home from Germany and we were attempting to reconcile our marriage because it had been a strenuous eighteen months for me with him being away. It was then that Pastor Caines told me that I didn't have a real marriage, and that I needed to bring my husband in before he would condone us living as husband and wife.

My husband refused to go before him, although we agreed that our marriage had become turbulent due to his absence, but he didn't understand why he needed the permission of the church to reconcile with his own wife. We decided we would put more effort toward living as husband and wife. I wouldn't allow him to come home when he returned because I was counseled against it. One night I was sitting at home reading "How to Stop the Other Woman from Stealing Your Husband" by Apostle Louis S. Greenup and I felt like I needed to give my marriage the chance to be what it should have been had my husband not went to Germany.

As I read the book I started to cry and wanted to see my husband against Pastor Caines advice.

I called my husband and expressed my desire to see him, so we got together and the next thing I knew a home pregnancy test revealed we were pregnant. As soon as I found out I called Pastor Caines to tell him the good news, I was happy about having another baby.

If you were wondering where Pastor Reed was, he was counseling people as well and away on speaking engagements. There is no rhyme or reason to how a member gets a particular Pastor. Each member for the most part has a

Pastor they are more comfortable with or referred to and they will direct all inquiries to that Pastor.

All I ever really wanted to do was to have children and be married. When I was younger both of my Fallopian Tubes were blocked and I had to have surgery in order to conceive, years later on I took 1 shot of the Depo-Provera for birth control and it sterilized me. I then had to go back to the fertility doctor in order to conceive my third child. So since I always had problems in the past getting pregnant this was great news, it has been 10 years since my last baby. I always wanted a large family, six children to be exact.

Well, to my surprise when I told my Pastor Caines he had me come into his office to meet with him at once. We talked an hour and a half about the next steps. He made it quite clear that he was not happy about the pregnancy.

"He told me I was a whore",

"Yes, my pastor said that to me!"

I was angry with him and told him he had no right to speak to me with such language. He told me that I didn't need any more children because I already had four and was thirty five years old. By this time I was so mentally controlled by him that I got over the comment he made about calling me a whore and bought into the reasoning that he only had my best interest at heart, and that he was protecting me!

Anyway when I called my husband to tell him we were expecting; he was shocked. He didn't think it would happen quite so soon and really didn't know what to say.

Pastor Caines was persistent in telling me that I didn't need any more children, he even went as far as to tell me that I had better terminate the pregnancy. He asked, "Why would you want to tie yourself down with another baby to a husband you barely knew".

Now I am really confused.

I thought this would be good for my marriage, but Pastor Caines thought differently, he said this was a bad idea.

I found myself in agony struggling with what to do next. When I went to the doctor they confirmed I was pregnant. Pastor Caines said I had his full support and convinced me that terminating the pregnancy would be the right thing to do, so I took his "Pastoral" advice and terminated the pregnancy.

I cried the entire way home, "What have I done!

What did I just do? I cried out to myself!

When I told my husband I terminated the pregnancy he was hurt, he said he wanted us to have a family together. I had never voluntarily terminated a pregnancy before and afterwards I felt so guilty.

Well, I went running back to see Pastor Caines he said, "I did a good thing because I didn't need any more children." Then the more he counseled me the more he kept telling me that I needed to divorce my husband. My husband and I were already not living together at this time, now after terminating the pregnancy things were surely looking bleak between us. I didn't know what to do. Pastor Caines and I spoke on the phone every day, several times a day. At this point he was dominating the direction in which my life was going and decided I needed to just divorce my husband and move on with my life. So in November 2005 I contacted a divorce center and

filed for divorce, six weeks later we were divorced. I was so brainwashed that I got my husband to sign the papers without even realizing what they were, he didn't even know we were divorced.

Time went on; the Holidays were here, for my children and I it was the first Holiday in our new home! I can remember Pastor Caines calling me on Christmas Eve; he was ironing curtains and hanging up Christmas decorations at his house. He even told me he decorated one of his Christmas trees my favorite color, "Purple."

Wow, did I feel special.

7

"My Soul was Rocked!"

*I*t was January 26, 2007 and I sent this email to my pastor.

Hey Good Morning Pastor Caines,

Last night I got in around midnight (working late in the office) I gave my daughter her fundraiser packet and went to bed. Around 5:30 am she woke up and came into my room and told me she couldn't sleep - I told her, "okay it's almost time for you to get up anyway". She began to break out and cry so I asked her what was wrong, she said she had a bad dream - I was frustrated because I was tired so I said okay go back to sleep. She said, Mommy I dreamed something happened to you. I said in an irritated tone "What, what happened to me?" She said, "You Died, and me and brother were all alone!"

MY SOUL WAS ROCKED!

I instantly felt sick, scared, and nervous and wanted to cry myself. As she stood in my doorway I preceded to tell her how, God forbid something happens to me, I have taught you and your brother what you need to know to survive. I told her I have no control over that, I am working out, eating right, etc. I told her that if something were to happen to mommy, that I wanted her to promise to always stay in touch with her brother and sisters (they would be with their father's). It hit me I am the glue to keeping my children together otherwise they could grow up in separate homes and possibly not ever see one another again.

Oh my God, Lord you have my undivided attention. I do not want to have my life taken away prematurely and leave my children all alone and divided.

Something else I thought about was not once did I say to her, baby come here - hold her in my arms and tell her baby, it's going to be alright. I believed both you and Pastor Reed when you said you can't show love if you've never been loved. It hit me. My own mother never hugged me or showed me that type of love and nurturing and I struggle with not being able to give that to my children. I PRAYED!

Yesterday, my broker and I had a long conversation and he told me that he had been observing, and studying me from a distance. He said "You want to be loved so bad by a man that if the wrong one comes along and says and does all the right things you will let him in your space - you will really get hurt."

Then he said, "You trust me;

You really trust me.

You trust me more than you trust yourself,

Why?

Know you to trust you."

Then he asked, when you go to the amusement park you have to pay to play the game to win the prize. So why do you give away your prize without anyone working for it or paying for it? I told Pastor Caines, "that it has never been about a price for me. I never knew it meant that much or was that special - The Cookie".

How do I change that thought process so that I can bring value and virtue to myself and my children.

I then asked, "Why"

Pastor Caines, "Why am I like this I don't know what to do?

I need your help and guidance;

I am open for your instruction."

On January 20, 2006 I had a conversation with an old friend of mine from Trenton who works for the Department of Commerce. He said to me, "I know you have so much love to give.....I continue to pray that a strong, confident, Passionate / sensual God-fearing man (that captures your interest-most important) is brought your way...he has to be able to 'Lead' you in the proper way, and not be intimidated by you." I said yes, I would like that, someone who will protect me, nurture and such - who loves the Lord and will teach me.

He said, "I see...just keep in mind....having been honored enough to have experienced your wit and passions...I believe that is no small order!

Roughly a couple of weeks later I went to see Pastor Caines for counseling– when I went to leave… normally my exit is that he would give me a hug good-bye. I had given him an Oscar style Accountability Award for his commitment and being influential in my life.

This one day he just kissed me.

The Pastor put his tongue down my throat.

I mean the kiss was pretty sloppy and wet too. Nobody kisses like that anymore. I don't think, at least I don't think. Nevertheless, he thrust his tongue right down my throat. I was like, "Oh My God!

I was shocked!

I just kind of put my head to the floor, looked at the floor and walked out.

I said nothing.

I didn't discuss it.

I didn't even talk about it.

I would call Pastor Caines for my counseling concerns and we would still talk on the phone and I would still go in for my monthly meetings with him, every three to four weeks to be exact. I felt violated however I just never felt comfortable enough to confront him about it.

During our counseling sessions he would read the Bible to me, he knew the bible so well that he read it while it was facing me and it being upside down to him. He was very professional and never let on that he was interested in me, not even after the kiss did he talk about it.

I was confused, my Pastor had kissed me, he put his tongue right down my throat, yes my Pastor!

I know I did not dream it, but nothing makes sense.

It's almost like being Alice in Wonderland.

Things were not as they seemed.

I even attempted to date other men, but Pastor Caines would not even hear of that. I couldn't keep a secret from him or tell him a lie. He knew me so well, he could tell if I was walking, sitting, standing, or resting; in a store, in the street, in a restroom, or eating while on the phone with him, He was very attentive!

… He would say... "Renee, what are you …." and he would be right on. Renee is my middle name.

He even did a Personality Profile on me and this is what the results showed:

SHANNON BELLAMY PERSONALITY TYPE

Your personality is **Choleric Sanguine**

Melancholy Strength:2 Weakness:1

8%

Phlegmatic Strength:3 Weakness:1

10%

Sanguine Strength:7 Weakness:8

38%

Choleric Strength:8 Weakness:10

45%

PERSONALITY TRAITS DEFINED

Sanguine A person who is sanguine is generally light-hearted, fun loving, a people person, loves to entertain, spontaneous, leader abilities, and confident. However they can be arrogant, cocky, and indulgent. She/he can be day-dreamy and off-task to the point of not accomplishing anything and can be impulsive, possibly acting on <u>whims</u> in an unpredictable fashion. Sanguine are motivated by people. This is great! Sanguine make people feel special because they are always so happy to see you and so interested in what is going on in your life. Sanguine don't care for rules and will often try to charm their way out of having to submit to them. So they need a good understanding of God's authority to keep them from taking it too far.

Choleric A person who is choleric is a doer. They have a lot of <u>ambition,</u> <u>energy,</u> and <u>passion.</u>The Choleric likes to take charge. It does not come from a prideful heart as some believe; it comes from a true leadership gift that God placed there. A Choleric can observe a situation and develop a plan and see it through to completion. The Choleric is not heartless and insensitive although they may appear that way to the untrained eye. The problem is that they say what is on their mind. To them, words do not carry a lot of weight. They can cast off bad comments and insults quickly and can often have a hard time understanding why others can't. Sticks and stones don't seem to harm the Choleric, and they probably don't. But, the Choleric one devastation is being misunderstood and considered emotionally cold. Don't believe that for a minute. There is a heart under there and it loves and wants to be loved, even if they can't easily show it.

<u>The Choleric/Sanguine</u> is great! They can get the job done and make sure everyone is having fun at the same time! They are extremely loyal to those who appreciate and encourage them.

Melancholic A person who is a thoughtful pondered has a *melancholic* disposition. Often very kind and considerate, melancholic's can be highly creative – as in <u>poetry</u> and <u>art</u> - but also can become overly pre-occupied with the <u>tragedy</u> and <u>cruelty</u> in the world, thus becoming depressed. A *melancholic* is also often a perfectionist, being very particular about what they want and how they want it in some cases. This often results in being unsatisfied with one's own artistic or creative works and always pointing out to themselves what could and should be improved. They are often loners and most times choose to stay alone and reflect.

Phlegmatic While phlegmatic are generally self-content and kind, their shy personality can often inhibit <u>enthusiasm</u> in others and make themselves lazy and resistant to <u>change</u>. They are very consistent, relaxed, rational, curious, and observant, making them good administrators and diplomats. Like the <u>sanguine</u> personality, the phlegmatic has many friends. However the phlegmatic is more reliable and <u>compassionate</u>; these characteristics typically make the phlegmatic a more dependable friend.

8

"Monica Lewinsky T-shirt"

I t's April 23, 2006, wow my life has taken a crazy twist. My real estate broker had been paying my rent since I moved to South Jersey out of my commissions. He paid all of my bills and just held on to the rest of my money. I didn't like paying bills; I always made lots of money and spent it well but I wanted my husband to "pay" the bills; since I had become very close to my broker I asked him and he said he didn't mind paying them. Every month I would bring in an envelope with my bills in it and hand it to him; I wouldn't follow up whether they were paid or not. I was making money so fast I couldn't even keep up. I thought my money would be safe if he just held onto it. Well, something went terribly wrong and I was notified by mail that I had to come to court. I was being evicted from my home for non-payment. I went to my broker and asked what happened to my money and why hadn't he paid my bills and he said, "he didn't have it." Didn't have it! What the !@#$? What does that mean I didn't have it, what happened to my money? He just said he didn't have it. Now what do I do, I have another closing in three weeks but how is that going to help me now. I am mad as !@#$, he said he will increase my commission to make up for my missing money. I'm angry but what can I do? If I leave his office with deals in the pipeline he doesn't have to give me my commission then I will surely be up a river without a paddle. God had to teach me a lesson....he taught me to be a "good steward" over what he has "given me" and the value of having money to be able to "pay my bills".

I am stuck!

Haven't I been through enough?

Why it is every man I allow to get close to me takes advantage of me?

Why? Now:

➢ I have 72 hours to move.

➢ I have to pack up a 3,000 sq. ft. home.

➢ I'm devastated.

➢ I have no family here.

➢ I am Homeless!

➢ What am I going to do?

I called a few of the real estate agents I was close to, to help me pack up my house. I had to put my things in storage. I knew I had a few closings coming up in a couple of weeks, but that was not going to help me right now. I called the church for help and they told me "No", they could not do it. I had faithfully tithed off of my real estate earnings. As much money as I have tithed in the last nine months, I mean thousands of dollars. I couldn't believe they said no. Wow!

I was evicted and had to be out by March 21st; everybody is coming over from my real estate office to help me pack up all my things to put in storage. I was running out of money, I called my family and they did what they could do however, I still ran out of money and needed more boxes. As I previously stated I did call the church administration office first. I think in February I had contacted the church after I had been there for a while and tithing on a regular basis and asked them for some assistance. I was having trouble paying my utility bills at this point because real estate was very slow over the winter. The church did pay some utility bills for me once; to those companies directly.

I ask the church for the security deposit. I had found another place to move to. I knew I had a closing coming up. The church told me "no". The church said they only help people once a year, but literally, my children and I are going to be homeless, I stated. We literally had no money. .What happened to my money only my broker knows, and that's another story for another time. The church said sorry, that they only help people once a year. This multi-million dollar church would only help their members once a year; even if they were tithing as much money as I had in such a short period of time. I finally broke down and called Pastor Caines, he had been my counselor for eight months now and we were close, like a counselor and counselee would be. I asked him if he could at least help me buy some more boxes, I'm going to put all of my things in storage and I'm going to split my family up for the time being. I'm distraught because I didn't know what I was going to do.

Pastor Caines said yes, he and his wife would come and buy me some more boxes. That Monday "he" came to my home in Sicklerville. He took me to buy some boxes in his SUV. He came back to my house to help me pack up the remainder of my things. I didn't think twice about him being there after all he was my Pastor, my confidant, my support. I was so upset and I'm crying because my children and I are being separated, all my things are going into storage.

I have never been homeless in my entire life, I felt so humiliated betrayed and disgusted.

I remember I was in the basement packing up my children's toys and other things and I was upset and crying, he walked over to comfort me, I thought, but he kissed me and the next thing I knew we were on the floor having sex. I don't remember a lot about the encounter except the fact that at that point I was upset and I was crying and just knew he was on top of me. Suddenly, my doorbell rang, it startled us! It was one of the real estate agents from my office, she came in and she saw my t-shirt was a mess. My clothes were all out of place.

> His semen was all over my t-shirt.
> Yes, he ejaculated on my shirt.
> No he wasn't wearing a condom.
> She saw the mess on my shirt.
> I was startled and acting all ditzy.
> I didn't even know what to say or what to think.
> I just didn't think anything.
> Even though I was repulsed by it, I did nothing!

I needed three storage units because my house was so big and I had so many things. So she picked me up and brought me to get another storage unit. She put one of the storage bins in her name. After I introduced them she and I went to the storage facility and he left to pick up his daughters from school.

Once the transaction was complete she left, she just dropped me off at my house, and she didn't even come back into the house. She knew something was wrong, she left immediately. She knew something had gone terribly wrong between him and I. When I walked back into the house I just sat on the stairs in my empty house and thought to myself, what the heck just happened? How could that have happened, and why?

> Did he just take advantage of me in my vulnerability?

I did what Monica Lewinsky did, I bagged the t-shirt with his semen intact I put it in a plastic bag for DNA evidence in the event he denied what had happened between us.

During this time I was attending the Biblical Institute at Sharon Baptist Church. I was studying to get my certificate in Christian Leadership. My teacher, Pastor Larry Stephens who was the brother-in-law of Pastor Keith W. Reed Sr. taught the class, news floating around that his ex-wife, Portia Busaitis protested in front of the church. She alleged that he sexually molested her deaf daughter; his stepdaughter of 12 years. Mrs. Busaitis personally spoke to me and states, "that the sexual abuse was not alleged by substantiated by the State of Delaware, the Department of Services for Children, Youth and their Families on December 3, 2003. She has a letter in which she showed me that states that the investigation concluded on July 30, 2003, substantiated the case for Sexual Abuse involving intercourse with "Mrs. Busaitis's minor daughter" by Larry Stephen. Mrs. Busaitis also stated that the protest in front of the church began because despite her reporting the crime to the then Senior Pastor Reed (now Bishop) and Church Board, he continued to allow Pastor Stephen to oversee the Educational Ministry and counsel female members at Sharon Baptist Church. Pastor Stephens now has his own church in Delaware, which includes a daycare facility." I called one of the students who I was friends with and told him to tell the Pastor Stephens that I am not coming back to class – nor am I coming back to Sharon anymore. After that encounter with Pastor Caines at my house I didn't know how to respond. I was confused and upset; I just said I wasn't going back to the church ever again. The student that I told went to class that night and told Pastor Stephens that I wasn't coming back. Pastor Stephens regularly joked calling me Pastor Caines girl in class; he knew Pastor Caines was my counselor. Pastor Stephens called me and asked me what was wrong and why wasn't I coming back, he said "you're a good student, an A student, what happened?" He said, "I love the babes (meaning new Christians), I love the babes in Christ, tell Pastor Stephens what happened. I felt that I could give him the benefit of the doubt and tell him the truth. He seemed to be a good teacher and Pastor from what I could see despite what I heard. I proceeded to tell him what had taken place between Pastor Caines and I. He didn't know how to deal with it. He didn't know what to say. So I found out later when I received the call from Senior Pastor Reed that Pastor Stephens had informed him of the incident.

I told Pastor Stephens that I felt like Pastor Caines had taken advantage of me;

that he manipulated me,

I felt violated and confused.

How is it that my Pastor/Counselor could have sex with me, and how could I have allowed it, this was not something that had crossed my mind no time did I feel like anything inappropriate was going on.

I was extremely upset and confused.

I felt betrayed.

Pastor Reed called me the next day. I remember exactly where I was when he called and how I was feeling. I was at my office manager's house; I was living from house to house at this time. My children were separated from me because we were homeless. I spoke to him on the phone and told him that I was confused and upset that this had taken and that I didn't understand why. I told him I was new in the faith and very distraught over this. He said okay and that he would deal with it.

He is the Senior Pastor and is responsible for his pastors and their conduct. At no point in the conversation with me did he ever bring up additional counseling with him or any other plan of action for me to cope with what happened. I thought Pastor Reed would be concerned about my mental, emotional, psychological or spiritual stability. However, he never showed that type of concern and I never saw any action taken. He only said he would deal with it, he never said how.

From what I understand according to Pastor Caines, Pastor Reed dealt with it by cursing him out and handing his ass to him in a sling, he so eloquently stated to me. The next day Pastor Caines called me and asked,

"Why did you tell?"

He was angry that I told.

He said, "Why didn't you come to me, if you were unsure or confused, why didn't you talk to me?"

Sure that was easy for him to say. I'm trying to figure out if I was abused or taken advantage of.

Ain't that just nothing…how you could go to your abuser and tell him you're confused about the fact that he forced himself on you. I had no idea what his reaction would be.

He was upset that I did not confide in him about the fact that I had difficulties about what had taken place. Pastor Reed never reached out to me to help me manage what had happened, so Pastor Caines did. He stepped up and convinced me that what he did was in my best interest. I was so grateful.

He said, "Ok, I'll walk you through it."

Pastor Caines always told me that he was responsible for my Holistic well being, and that he is here for me holistically. That was his word, "Holistically". He even used the Bible to justify what he had done.

He actually told me "his version" of the story of David in the Bible, and how:

> David was a man of God,
> That if only David had asked God for Bathsheba he would have given her to him,
> That is what David did, but not who he was,
> He said he asked God for me,
> God would "allow" it, but not condone it. What did that mean? My vulnerabilities at that time allowed him to tell me anything.

He was consistently telling me things about the Bible to justify what he had done, making it seem alright and allowable by God but just not accepted.

Does that mean:

> God will allow it but not condone it?

Huh, though it seems crazy he made it make sense! I fell for it, Hook Line and Sinker! He seemed so sincere! He seemed like he really wanted nothing but the best for me and my children, he articulated things so well! He "always" prayed with me. He was not afraid to thank God while with me therefore, I believed in my mind that he must've known what he was talking about. Of course he did, he was a Pastor. He was used and favored by God.

9

"He's good for me, he's what I need"

then love crept in....

astor Caines apologized to me.

He said he was sorry and he only gave me what he thought I needed. I'm losing my home, my children are not with me and that's what I need!

Wow, I don't know when I've ever heard that what a person "needs" when going through tribulations is to have sex with their Pastor, but ooookay.....

He said he thought I was grown enough and ready to handle him.... He told me that he is not cheap with himself and wouldn't sleep with every woman who comes into his office. Wow, I guess I should feel privileged. He bragged about the amount of women in the church who wanted him, but claimed he refused them. About three weeks had gone by since that first encounter. He called me countless times working on my mind to convince me that is was okay, that he was good for me, and this (he) was what I need for my life to progress and move to the next level.

On the Wednesday after Easter, I went to his office for my regular counseling session. I'm not sure why I decided to continue my sessions looking back but that I was brainwashed. During the session he told me he hadn't had lunch, and he was interested in grabbing a bite to eat with me. He asked me to pick up lunch and meet him at the park not too far from the church.

Pastor Caines and I had a picnic in the park.

He said later that evening he wanted to get together to talk, but later that evening I received a call from him saying he had to cancel because he was needed at home.

The next morning he surprised me and was at my door. I knew that was trouble.

When he walked in the door, I admit he had this certain sexiness about him, with that bowlegged stroll to his walk, smelling nice with a black linen suit on…. As he walked in the door Mary Mary "Yesterday" was playing, (the jazzy version) now every time I hear it I see Pastor Caines walking through the door.

He captured my heart…I was weak.

He told me that what we have is precious…

I believed him…

Protect it and protect him…I said I would.

He seemed vulnerable.

He said he loved me, and I began feeling an obligation to do just that - protect it and him. The head game worked. Didn't I feel guilty about his wife and family? No I didn't. That was not my responsibility. He came to me. He deceived me and He said he never lied to her. He loves me and cares for me and my children. That is what he tells me. We love each other and it is a "Spiritual" love, so God will allow it, he said. He has invested in my soul, mind, body, and children. He said all the right things. The afternoon was beautiful, I cooked, we drank, and he made it beautiful. Though it was wrong it was beautiful. He introduced me to "Riesling"; it's his favorite white wine from Johannesburg. He began to fix anything that needed to be fixed; he did repairs on the house and even hung my chandelier. He was that person, that man every woman waits for…that man. He did everything. I couldn't even imagine allowing anyone else to make love to me, what a beautiful and passionate exchange between us. He looked into my eyes and whispered my name…"ohh Ms. Bellamy."

Wow! Life has been so crazy; it's been about a month, Pastor Caines came over today from 3-9:30 pm. Today must have been the 6th time we've made love, it is more beautiful every time and I have grown to love him so much. That whisper drives me crazy!

He is very passionate…

He whispers in my ear…

Ms. Bellamy…

He calls me his "Longtail". Pastor Caines is from Bermuda, he said Longtail is the name of a beautiful bird there, and their emergence symbolizes the beginning of the tourist season. The islanders know its money, money, money time…

My time with him is so beautiful; today he came and fixed the closet rails, and crept up behind me while I was kneeling in the recliner looking out the window in my bedroom. He started caressing and kissing my neck and then pulled my panties off and lead me to the bed and started making love to me. He is so passionate when he touches me; I guess it is wrong however, he says its right! He said he will do wrong – Right! No man has ever treated me the way he does. He listens to me, and he has taken his time to get to know me and my desires – he does love me, he claimed infatuation, but it had to be more. He is strong and very grown at 52 years of age, but I know that I am penetrating his heart and being. Am I infecting his Soul or is he infecting mine? We made love continuously for about 2 hours, we hugged, kissed, caressed, he sang to me and kissed me on my forehead, he is so sweet. He whispers in my ear and calls me by my name, "Shannon Bellamy", and then he calls me sweet. He looks at me in awe; I have told him that I love him, my love for him is very grown, it is neither lust nor infatuation, he has earned my love – he said he had no idea he would be the recipient of the new Shannon Bellamy, but he is glad he is the one.

I wonder how will it end or is this just the beginning.

I cooked dinner for him and made two new drinks called the *"Caines" and the "Shannon"*, Shannon had watermelon flavor, mango flavor, lemon liqueur, sprite and Grand Marnier. The Caines was the same except for the Watermelon, Grand Marnier, and sugared rim. I always give him something to think about.

The Real Estate market had begun to slow down, so I moved my office furniture out of my broker's office and brought it home. He has really been acting like an ass, like someone needs him. His office in Sicklerville may not survive if he continues to be cheap and not put more money in marketing. He just reduced my salary for marketing. He is full of "Sugar Honey, and Ice Tea", pretending to care…how am I supposed to make a living or pay my rent. I am his top selling agent in a regular market, and I do more than just sell real estate, I do administrative and marketing for the company as well.

Anyway by this time Pastor Caines and I are talking every day, and he is making weekly trips to my house. I can't have another man, because as he said, "He is My Man!"

10

"Was I Poisoned, I can't Breathe?"

ack around early May there was a gospel concert at church, and I decided to go with Tiffany, who was another member from Sharon Baptist Church, and also a Registered Nurse. I had become close to her while attending the Sharon Baptist Biblical Institute. As we sat there watching the concert, Pastor Caines came onto the stage with the rest of the pastors. Tiffany saw me blushing and said, girl do tell, you like the Pastor. I said, girl, well - I am seeing one of them. She guessed the right one the first time.

After the concert she invited me out for dinner, it was a belated birthday dinner for me. She said your choice of restaurant. Hmmm, I have never been to "Tangerine" in Center City, Philadelphia, Pa. it's pretty and I would love to go there. I followed her to the restaurant in my car.

SOMETHING MYSTERIOUS HAPPENED THAT NIGHT!

I ordered one drink; while I was waiting for my drink I excused myself and went to the ladies room. When I returned my drink was there, we talked, laughed and ate dinner. I had one drink; it was I believe something peachy. It was a small glass and I only had one. But by the end of the night I couldn't drive home.

Tiffany offered to leave her car in Center City and drive my car to her house and let me stay the night. She had one drink as well but she was fine. Hmmm, I remember being slightly conscious while she was driving me to her house. I remember her saying; you are so pretty, I am so jealous of you. I was in and out of consciousness. I also can remember my head hanging over the seat and her talking but I couldn't make out what she was saying because I was so out of it. When we got to her house she said I could sleep on the sofa till morning. I didn't even have a blanket or anything; I just tried to sleep off whatever it is that had me like that. I am not a drinker I had my first drink at the age of 34, and even now I am a social drinker.

The next morning when I woke up my throat was feeling scratchy. Tiffany and I went to get her car and then went to breakfast at the Marriott Hotel. She started asking me questions about the relationship between Pastor Caines and me. She was disturbed, and told me that the relationship between him and I was inappropriate and that I needed to stop seeing him. The conversation began to get intense, so I finished breakfast and went on with my day.

Physically, I felt progressively worse as the day went on. By late afternoon I had to be rushed to the hospital, my throat felt like someone had slit it! I went to the emergency room and the doctors said I had some type of poison in my body and gave me a strong antibiotic to combat it. A few weeks went by and I realized that I hadn't spoken to Tiffany.

That day I cried. What happened to me?

On Monday, June 5; I found out that Tiffany told Pastor Stephens, who was our teacher in our Tithing class and her counselor about me and Pastor Caines. Pastor Stephens had already known, he was the one I reported it to the first time it happened; the time I felt violated. Then the following Sunday she walked up to Pastor Reed at the end of the service and told him as well, but Pastor Reed already knew! Had he addressed the issue when he first heard about it maybe the outcome would have been different and I might not be writing this book.

Pastor Caines is furious with me, he said I betrayed him. I could kill Tiffany – if I had it in my heart ….Thank God for Jesus. I hate her for mentioning it to Pastor Reed. However, I 'm partly to blame I told her and thus gave her the key to a very special place inside of me, a place that was 'precious to me'. Self destruction is what Pastor Caines called it. He said, "How could you give away something that so was precious to you?"

I can't breathe.

I need Jesus to heal me.

I have repented over and over again; but I can't let go!

Pastor Caines has exiled me from his life. He is very guarded now with me. I have matured so much; this was a big girl lesson. I am in love with my Pastor and he is hurt and running for his life, back to his place of refuge….his wife.

It took a minute for him to cool off and forgive me. He started calling me all over again, and told me I had to learn a lesson but that he loved me and that if this is precious to me then I need to protect it and protect him.

Over the last three months (summer) my children were away, and it was then that "Glenn" (now I was calling

Pastor Caines "Glenn" – his first name…when not at church) and I spent countless days together, he got away for 8 hours on a Monday, he came over every single week. We even got it in inside of my coupe the day of the Spirit of Philadelphia Cruise for Real Estate professionals in New Jersey.

He called me the morning of the boat cruise and said he wanted to see my dress before I left. He slipped away and we met in a supermarket parking lot not too far from his house. He said he ran out of the house with just some shorts and a t-shirt on! EZ access…..

After a short while we parted ways and I went to catch the boat cruise.

While I was on the Spirit of Philadelphia, he and his wife went to the Caribbean Fest on Penn's Landing in Philadelphia, Pa. He left me a message on my cell phone saying, "When I saw your boat go under the bridge… a part of me was on the boat inside of you." He said, although he was at the Caribbean feast with "other" people he was thinking about me! Gotta love this man, He is so spontaneous.

I'm all in by this time….

He says it, I do it! It's snowing in July…

And I am putting on boots.

About 4 weeks later, I go with Mia to get my eyelashes done. Mia was another sister from the church; she was one of Pastor Reed's favorite "counselees", or so I've been told.

After we were done at the Eyelash Bar on Germantown Avenue, in Philadelphia, (two twin brothers own) she invited me to come to a party with her at the Blue Martini. I went home to change my clothes and I went back to pick up Mia. Mia sang on the choir. I have never seen a woman with a size 28 inch waist and 60 inch hips and pretty…. She is beautiful and can work a weave, her hair is always tight and right, and her voice is softer than mine, oh, and can dresssss. Mia has eight children, even though she's in a self described rocky marriage.

Mia and I went to a party at the Blue Martini in Ole' City that night, her friend, his wife and homeboy went – they had some extra stuff going on in the parking lot, then they invited me to a swingers party and told me "no panties" were allowed. I told Glenn (Pastor Caines) about the evening. He forbid me to go, and therefore I didn't think twice about it, I didn't go!

Mia came out and asked me if I was seeing Pastor Caines, when I didn't answer she said she knew, she said that she has been around him when I've walked into the room and he would say hmm, there goes my baby. He didn't even realize that she had heard him. She told me that she discerned that Glenn and I were together –

She said that if I ever told her business…

She would tell Pastor Reed;

Little did she know he already knew!

11

"He said I was Good for his Prostate"

hings between Pastor Caines and I were peaceful, and Real estate was booming again. I was financing breakfast, lunch, dinner, and his expensive vitamin list, whatever he asked for he got it. He told me that he went to the doctor six months ago and the doctor said he needed to take better care of himself, and that his prostate was showing some signs of being weak. Huh, he came back to me six month later and told me that doctor asked him what he was doing differently because his prostate was functioning perfectly! He laughed... and said I (Madame Duchess) was good for a brotha's prostate ....check out the email for yourself:

Hey Babe:

Here is the list as promised

1. Lycopene - 30 mg
2. MegaMen 50 plus
3. Korean Ginseng - 100 mg
4. Cranberry - 500 mg
5. L - Arginine 500 - 500 mg
6. Beta Sitoterol
7. Selenium
8. Garlique or (Garlic -1000 mg)

I really appreciate you looking out for me. My system has become so accustomed to a routine. With your help I have been able to maintain so well. I have been feeling so good lately. I believe with the pace I at which move, failing to administer my "daily concoction" my body reacts.

I have gotten so into this rhythm, my body now sees it as normal. Any deviation throws me off my thing!

So Madame Duchess, get me back on in every way. I need my nurse...

Thanks for being and becoming you...

12

He said,

"I would look good with a set of Twins"

I was rolling in the dough again. Now here comes the talk about body enhancement. We discussed Breast Augmentation and he said that it would be a great look for me. He sent me information about cosmetic surgeons and I did my own research as well to find a doctor I was comfortable with. After ten consultants with cosmetic surgeons in New Jersey and Philadelphia, I settled on Dr. Adrian Lo in Philadelphia, PA. Dr. Lo was the tenth doctor I consulted with, because he had the best bedside manner of them all, and his office staff was unparalleled and very helpful. I told Pastor Caines I had settled on a surgeon. The time came to have my first cosmetic procedure. My girlfriend drove me to the hospital because had some issues going on at the time; one being his grandda severely pre-mature and struggling to live. Unfortunately she later passed away right around the same time I was having my breast augmentation surgery and he told me he needed money so I went to the church and dropped off an envelope for him of $300.00. He called and gave me the information for the funeral services, and I was sore from my surgery but wanted to be there for him, so I went to the funeral services for his granddaughter. I went to the church and sat in the back. He saw me, I didn't speak to anyone, and after the service I went straight home. I had just come out of the hospital after having my surgery.

When I woke up from my procedure he was there with my girlfriend to see me off safely. I was so sore and sleepy. I can remember him telling me that I was beautiful, and kissing me on the forehead. My girlfriend drove me home. What a ride that was. It was raining really hard and the streets were all bumpy and my breast was already hurting like the dickens. When I got home I went straight to bed with my Percocet in hand.

My son and daughter took care of me that night. My oldest daughter who was 13 years old at the time slept in my room and got up all through the night to help me to the bathroom, and get me water and pain medication as I needed it. The next day I laid in the recliner in my room all drugged up and feeling bad. I can remember my girlfriend Tanya calling to check on me and my words were so slurred that she just asked to speak to one of my children and told them to tell me she called to check on me. The next day I stopped taking the Percocet because I realized I wasn't in pain, I was feeling sick. It was the drugs, so I called my doctor and he gave me Vicodin; that made me just as ill. I finally took myself off the Vicodin and just took some Extra Strength Tylenol. I felt so much better. Pastor Caines came over to see about me on day two. I can remember him kissing my sore new "twins"; and the next thing I know, yep, we were having sex.

Don't even ask!

He said he wanted to be there for me!

He was for all intents and purpose, "My Man". A few days later I was back on the mend; just a little slower than I am use to.

My girlfriends were all so mad. They all hated him. Especially Liz, she was very opinionated about my dealing with him. She was already mad because he was married, and a Pastor, but to make matters worse she knew I was spending my money and he wasn't doing anything for me. Then there was Vanessa, the Executive girlfriend. She stated her opposition and told me that she would be there to pick up the pieces when I got hurt from this situation. I can remember her asking "how is it that you're playing 2nd", she said,

"Shannon, I have never known you to settle for #2 in nothing, why now?" I've never been in a relationship with a married one. They are always propositioning me because they find me fascinating, but no. The answer is no.

I could not believe how he was able to move around so freely. I saw him more than I did the boyfriend I was dating, who was single. Sprint was both of our phone carriers. Sprint could show on the phone records numerous phone calls between the two of us. I just recently changed my phone to T-Mobile, but we had hundreds of thousands of phone calls between the two of us…we called each other all the time. If he was on vacation he would still call – one time he was in California, he sent his wife into the bank and called me while she was in the bank. He would be out with his family shopping and he would send the kids into the store so he could sit on the phone and talk to me. He maneuvered and manipulated so well. Another man could never cheat on me because I've seen him flow so well – he never missed a beat, he never, ever, missed a beat. I would talk to him every single day. A day didn't go by – unless his wife was sticking close by and then he would call me and tell me that he couldn't talk to me – "I'm not going to call so don't try to call me, I'll call you", he would say. I had his home phone number, and his home office phone number. I had full knowledge of everything, his comings and goings.

Every Sunday after church me and my kids would go down to the front of the church and say hello to him. He'd look at me; I mean look me over, to make sure I looked good to him. Then after church, once he was on his way home (he and his wife would always take separate cars) he would call me to tell me how beautiful I was that day, and say he'd see me tomorrow. This was consistent. So I would go to church, listen to the Pastors preach or listen to him preach. After church he would call me, and the next day we would have our rendezvous. And this was consistent. We would spend time together during the week. This went on, and on, and on until he just got so cocky, and comfortable with this double life that he put my life in danger and then made me feel like I was just worth nothing. That was the end. When everybody was saying "Shannon you need to get away", I couldn't see it. I honestly couldn't see it – as strong as I am, it was like I was under hypnosis. I was deep in it, yet I couldn't see it.

I would reiterate to her what Pastor Caines told me about being good for me and how much better my life would be with him in it. I stopped telling Liz early in the game because she, being from New York, wanted to confront him about taking advantage of me. Liz said she was going to tell the Bishop. And I said, "What are you going to tell him for, he knows." The Bishop knew. At this point I had talked to Pastor Reed, and told Pastor Reed that I was in love with this man. Pastor Reed said, "Oh, I can see how you love him." In my mind I was in love with this man. Pastor Caines became everything I ever wanted in a man. It was, by far, the best relationship I was ever in. He was everything to me. He was my Pastor, friend, my counselor, my confidant, handyman, companion and he was my lover. He spoke to me really nice. He was really good to me, or so I thought, all of this despite not paying my bills. I was the one spending all of the money in this relationship.

My bestfriend Vanessa, on the other hand, was privy to most of the dealings and conversations I had with him. I would even tell her some of the negative comments Pastor Caines would make to me, and she would say, "Why do you let him talk to you like that?" "Like what?" I would say? I couldn't see it. I had on "Rose Colored Glasses"

13

My Pastor was sent for Business...

But he... invited me for Pleasure

Marriott's Frenchman's Reef
St. Thomas, US Virgin Islands

$\mathcal{P}$astor Caines invited me to St Thomas, he had to go there for business...wedding business. Well September 12, I flew to St. Thomas to meet him, we spent six days in St. Thomas, it was magical – he was the perfect gentlemen.

Four weeks post-op from breast augmentation surgery, I'm swollen and I'm in St. Thomas. Huh, wondering how we pulled this off without "the wife", well he was asked to perform a wedding in St. Thomas. Since his wife had to work and couldn't get any time off until the weekend. He asked me to go, wow this was major exciting to me...it was like a movie. He originally asked me to come from Tuesday until Friday morning then his wife would arrive from Friday evening until Sunday. He was arriving on Wednesday. Well, he convinced her that it was not economical for them to spend that much money for just two and half days. The bride and groom had paid for his trip and weekend stay in St. Thomas. His plan was now set; with her safely tucked away at home we were free to enjoy a 6 day vacation, just the two of us. Oh yeah, wondering where the wedding party and guests were since most of them was from the church, they were at another hotel safely on the other side of the island.

He requested to be put up in a hotel away from the guests for the wedding since he is the "Pastor". Clever isn't he?

Day 1

My Arrival in St. Thomas

I need to bare my soul, my trip to St. Thomas. My flights were perfect; the connection to the hotel was uneventful. When I arrived I was so excited – the hotel (Frenchman's Reef & Morning Star Marriott Beach Resort) was more beautiful than I expected. I checked in the hotel for one night, of course I paid. The plan was for me to check into his room once he arrived. I went to my room but when I opened the door I felt "empty". I started to regret coming a day early. I was so lonely. I tried to call Glenn – I got no answer. I went to the pool and had lunch at the Sunset Café, huh no need to ask why they call it that, the view was breathtaking. The restaurants patio faced the ocean with a perfect view of the sunset. After I ate, I relaxed poolside then took a dip, well a float, I can't swim. I finally journeyed back to my room to try and call Glenn again, this time he answered. I immediately came alive. He gave me peace. He told me that he couldn't wait to get there and told me to enjoy myself until he did. I went back poolside, and then explored the hotel's amenities, by 9:30 pm I was in bed, I wanted to get to bed because I knew he would be here tomorrow and I wanted the time to hurry on by. I had a surprise for him when he arrived.

Day 2

Shopping...Quality Quality

I got up this morning and immediately rolled over and called Glenn praying all was well, and that he'd be at the airport. Happy was I when he told me he was waiting to, "Get his happy ass on the plane." I smiled, my heart was elated. I got dressed and told myself, "Girl go have fun, he wants you to." After I had breakfast, which was fabulous I might add I took a cab to the shopping district. It was pretty exciting. I tried on $10,000.00 - $20,000.00 rings and imaged what he would choose for me. I bought a little, but I didn't go crazy. The locals were losing their mind with their pick-up lines. One local vendor escorted me to the coconut man where I got a coconut opened it and drank the coconut water, I didn't like it though, but it was the Island thing to do. This one local man was very assertive about getting me a cab back to the hotel, he made me nervous. He said he would get his truck and take me wherever I wanted to go. When he went to fetch his truck I saw my hotel's ferry and I went for it. I wanted to be safe so I listened to my intuition. I didn't want to give the enemy no place to try to take my life. When I returned from shopping about 11:30am

I went back poolside eagerly anticipating Glenn's arrival. I decided to surprise him. I went to the front desk to check out of my room at noon. While at the counter two women walked up and was checking in, one said I have a reservation for "Caines" oh my – it's the bride and her wedding coordinator. The silly desk clerk told her his wife checked in yesterday. I was nervous that she was about to point me out. I had already explained to the desk clerk I was checking out of my room however, I would be joining my party once he arrived. I left the front desk and went to see the manager. I was livid – I told the manager that the clerk was telling my private business, and asked her to stop the clerk from divulging any more information. The manager said she would take care of it, and proceeded to do so, then apologized for the error and gave me the key to Glenn's room. Hmmmm, because of the clerk's big mouth it allowed me to get the keys to his room so that I could surprise him before he arrived. This was better than what I had planned.

The Rendezvous

I was able to set up! I went to "Our" room and unpacked and thought, girl set it up! I put candles all over, rose petals on the floor and bed, pulled out the Pina Colada warming oil, lingerie, Canoodle game, 269 sex play game, and sprayed the bed with perfume. Now that the ambiance was set I went back to the pool. Time seemed to be taking forever. Finally 3 pm came and I went to the lobby hoping he was there, to my surprise he was at the front desk! When I saw him at the counter I crept up behind him, he was as cool as a cucumber. We went up to the room. I did not let on that I had already been inside. He opened the door; the room was dark because the blinds were closed. When I opened the blinds he saw the roses and sexy setup. He smiled and said, "Oh my, you've been in the room", and he pulled me close to him and kissed me. Then he said "baby I am hungry." I thought to myself great! I had already ordered lunch to arrive for 5 pm. I called and had it brought up right away. We had Shrimp & Tequila Wraps, a fruit platter, Rum Runner and Sunsplash for lunch. Half way through lunch he Nailed me"!! The first of many!

Energizer Bunny

We made love three times before the night was over. Once he finished serenading me we showered and took a cab to Paradise Point. We took the Tram up to the restaurant on the top of the mountain. It was beautiful. We even danced. While we were having cocktails he said, "Would you like half a dance?" Yes I answered, he lead we danced. I was falling in love with him all over again. He wore a navy linen pant suit. He picked out my clothes that evening. I had on a brown & ivory sundress. When we left the restaurant we took the tram back down. On the way down we turned up the heat, yes, in less than five minutes. Once at the bottom we found a cab and went back to the hotel to continue what we got started. He's been on me like a "Young Buck".

Day 3

Quality Time

We woke up this morning, Bam! He's at it again, we almost missed breakfast, can't say he's not "on-top" of his game. I didn't think he had it in him at 52 years of age.

He's been assertively "Asserting"!

Today we went down to the shopping district. I enjoyed just strolling with him. It started raining so we stopped at a Café, he had a Long Island Ice Tea and I had Sex on the Beach. After the rain stopped we went to the Ferry and came back to the hotel, he is at it again! Damn, I can't keep up with him! Ewwh! Can a sista catch her breath? After he finally finished his physical therapy for his prostate we went to the beach. It was so stimulating to watch him in the ocean – so happy and carefree. Mr. Excited almost lost his glasses. He dove into the ocean with his glasses on, he realized when he came up that they were on and had fallen off in the ocean. He went back under about three times before he saw them lying on the ocean floor. I was nervous for him. Mr. Happy – he's so cute. We finally went back to the room.

We talked – I cried. This relationship and my insecurity about our future burden my heart. My question to God! Why? Why do you give me a perfect man that I'm not able to have totally for me? This pains me. Glenn and I had the opportunity to share, to and from each other's heart. Cut me open I am pink – the fear and uncertainty of not having him in my life consumes me. Well it's time for him to go to the wedding rehearsal. I went back to the pool. I came back to the room around 6:30pm; he was back by 7:30. We had dinner reservations at Havana Blue at 8pm, we were celebrating his birthday. I was so happy when he returned, I could breathe again. We got dressed, he picked out my brown strapless dress and Baby Phat sandals, and he had on a sexy beige and camel pantsuit. We went to Havana Blue Restaurant, the music was "Latin Groove", Oh my, the restaurant and ambiance was so sexy. We took some beautiful pictures, he looked so happy. Our table was next to the window, there was no glass, and we overlooked the ocean and white sand. I drank the Havana Blueberry and he had the Mango Mojito and Mango Papayatini. He was bent; he was so cute with it, all happy. He ate the Sea Bass and I had the Grouper, the food was fabulous, the ambiance was set in all white, only lit by candle light. So sexy it was. After dinner the waitress brought a chocolate cake with a candle for his birthday. We kissed, finished dessert and went back to the hotel and I put him to bed, those cocktails wiped out the little energizer bunny for me this time.

I tossed and turned all night, my breast hurt at night, my side is hurting as well, I am in so much pain but I am trying not to wake him.

Day 4

St. Thomas

What a morning, three times before 10 am, the little energizer bunny was all charged up after a good night sleep. We played canoodle this morning, it was sweet. What is canoodling? It is a game with cards and you have to ask or do to each other whatever the card says, it's a great way to break the ice and build communication and allow you to find out what your partner thinks about you. You know the things he normally doesn't tell you but recognizes. He had to give me a foot massage, lap dance, butterfly kiss, remove clothing with his mouth and he had to tell me three physical things he loves about me, he answered…eyes, mouth and teeth. The last card drawn I drew – it was, oh my, right up his alley, he's at it again. Then we cheated and the energizer bunny was back at it again, yes twice more! While making love to him by mistake I called him "Pastor Caines", wow! It turned me on even more. Have I lost my mind!

Two Phenomenal Women

We went to breakfast then to the beach, we talked, he barred his soul, or so he said! We shared our hearts, my soul cried. I love this man so. I watched him in the ocean, his smile lights up my heart. My spirit is crying and my heart can't take it, my inner being is confused. I asked him did he plan on leaving his family. He said he has no reason to. He told me he has sex with his wife and they don't argue. He said he loves us both. His wife, she is a phenomenal woman he says. He explained to me how they got together. He said, they were friends, great friends…after he had gone through a previous bad divorce and his ex-wife took his two children and moved away, it was his friend and now current wife who tracked them down. He said and for that he is eternally grateful and committed to her for it. He said they don't have any problems in their marriage. He said, his wife told him she didn't care what he did out in the street as long as it didn't hit her door. He said infidelity is no reason to end a marriage, and he told me he'd never lie to his wife in order to see me. It cut me down the center. He said having his wife and I was like having both Wachovia and Bank of America. They are great banks, great rates, and both have a great return, they are just different banks. He said he just happens to have Two Phenomenal Women because "he can". When I told him that if I were his wife "We" would be counseling folks, he said why, you don't trust a brother? Huh, his wife trusts him and allows him to counsel women and if she only knew her husband loves another woman. Then I said to him that his wife should be more vocal and visible in the church. He said, he told her it was "His Job" to counsel not hers. He said what's wrong with a woman being all she can be and not sitting under her husband. Huh, because he could be in an "extra-marital relationship" with his counselee, with a Shannon Bellamy – caught up!

The nerve.

Pastor Caines told me that he didn't have to stay in this affair – the point – that he is still doing it even after I have told four people, Pastor Stephens, then Pastor Reed, then Tiffany and Mia. He reinforced that he is a very private person, he got over it but he told me the others would have never said a word, you could turn their dress upside down and nothing would fall out.

He is so arrogant.

Pastor Caines claims, Pastor Reed is riding him because I divulged what had happened sexually between us. However, we were still in the relationship and Pastor Reed knew I was still seeing him. I told him. Pastor Reed and I exercised at the same gym. I sat down with him at L.A. Fitness and I told him…in Turnersville, New Jersey. I told Pastor Reed. I admitted that I was still seeing Pastor Caines. I said that things were good. I'm still in counsel with him, but the relationship is good. He said, "I can see how you could be attracted to him. I can see how you could love him because he is a very powerful and very smart man. I can see how." I said that I did not violate his family. Pastor Reed never took the initiative as being the head of that church to bring me into his office and say – Listen Shannon, what happened is not good, it's wrong, I don't condone it – you are here for spiritual well being and it's my responsibility to bring you in – I don't want you going to counseling with him anymore – I don't want you calling him. He never did any of that. He could have very easily, at that point, at inception, he could have easily stopped it by just bringing me in – constantly counseling me – constantly talking to me and helping me emotionally, physically and spiritually get back to a place of wholeness – there wouldn't have been a need for Pastor Caines. But Pastor Reed just left me out there, just let the ball drop and Pastor Caines has me sitting here dangling – I'm feeling suicidal – I don't know what to do. I feel violated. I feel used and abused.

This man became everything to me and now he's telling me to just stop. Don't do it anymore. I'm supposed to go home now and just be by myself, and pretend nothing happened? I'm distraught. Pastor Caines of course, he coerced me back into things; he made sure everything was happy and fuzzy. He's juggling. At this point he had things under control. I'm a chef as well. I gave him recipes. So he would take the recipes home and cook them for his wife. He never got busted because he would be at my house during the day. He would always leave my house in time to pick up his daughters from school. So he never missed school. He would pick up his kids everyday from school. He'd be at church, leave church and come to my house, spend time with me and go back to church and go to work or on Monday on his day off he would stay at my house until it was time to pick up his kids from school. He would pick up his kids from school. Go home and cook. By the time his wife got there he was looking like the perfect husband.

Every move his wife made, I knew about it. When she was sick and he couldn't talk he would let me know. He would call me and let me know that he would call me whenever he could. He would make late night milk runs to call me. So he would call me at 11 or 12 o'clock at night. Sometimes at 1 o'clock in the morning he would sneak out of the house to call me. He would call me while he was in the bathroom.

He was that man. It got to the point where I was so comfortable with him counseling me, and reading the bible with me. I was going out to dinner by myself. I was going to shows by myself. I was just waiting to see him. He was angry. He didn't want me seeing other people. He said, "If I'm your man and I'm supplying all of your needs what do you need somebody else for? I am holistically taking care of you." So he would always use that as a way to validate this relationship. He never, ever talked about leaving his wife. He never talked about leaving his family. He just wanted to have it, from the time I met him until our first intimate encounter. He told me later when things were good that he wanted to make sure that I could handle the relationship. He would have done it a lot sooner but he did not know if I was emotionally able to deal with it. So he acted and finally propositioned me when he thought that he had me totally at a place that I would totally be able to handle this situation.

Pastor Caines told me that Pastor Reed was not mad about our relationship, he was mad that I told. That you could take the other women and turn them upside down, nothing would ever fall out of their dresses. Why is it that I could not hold my mouth? That it's happened numerous times and nobody has ever told. He says I'm the first time his business has ever been out. He's never been accused of indiscretions because he was able to control the situation and that women never, ever told. So he was very comfortable. He knows that there had been other situations – like even with Pastor Robinson – everybody had known that Pastor Robinson was having sex with the people that he was counseling in the office, and Pastor Robinson finally quit and Pastor Reed knew that too. Pastor Robinson quit because he wanted to be with the other woman that he was counseling, he did leave his wife for her. Pastor Caines told me that Pastor Reed said to Pastor Robinson you can do what you do, but you can't leave your wife because of her, it makes the church look bad. Pastor Reed told him to either go back to his wife or you don't have a job. Pastor Robinson said he was not going back to his wife, so he quit and continued his illicit relationship with this other woman. The other woman said, "Hey, we can play but you can't live here." So now Pastor Robinson ended up going off with another woman. So he left his wife and went and stayed with another woman. And then he came back wanting his job back, but Pastor Reed would not give it to him. So Pastor Robinson went on about his business, and although his wife stayed at the church, his wife maintained her faith while he publicly embarrassed her, she danced so graceful in the Dance Ministry, she is one who has a special place in God's heart for her humility…God Bless her "100 fold", she deserves the desires of her heart…Pastor Robinson never came back.

His wife was still there as one of the first ladies. Then this same woman that Pastor Robinson was seeing – when he stopped seeing her, she started being counseled by Pastor Reed. I understand and she was going around openly saying she really wanted Pastor Reed. That he was hot and she really wanted him. And he counseled her for a while and all of a sudden, she left. So I don't know what became of her.

One time Pastor Caines and I were together and we went out to Delaware for the day. We went to the liquor store to pick up wine for his house and when we came back, his friend, Pastor Lambert – a former pastor at Sharon Baptist Church – was on the phone. Well Pastor Caines was calling Pastor Lambert for an alibi for the day, and Pastor Lambert was calling Pastor Caines for an alibi for the day. They were calling each other at the same time, so if either one of their wives called, they were with each other. Well, Pastor Lambert's wife subsequently found out about his affair. She went through his cell phone and retrieved a message from his woman, who happened to be his secretary. Allegedly Pastor Lambert was in a five-year affair with his secretary and when his wife learned of it she went to the board of trustees, and had her own husband (who was the senior pastor of that church), sat down. Then finally, after a year of him being sat down, his church let him go back to power. He allowed his ministry to discipline him publicly and was humbled by the experience. God has restored his life and ministry, His Grace & Mercy is everlasting. This was what they do, what many of them do. Pastor Lambert and Pastor Caines are very good friends. They are best buddies. However Pastor Lambert was not prideful or arrogant about his short comings.

My Heart Aches

I tried to be strong, but it hurts and confuses me even more. I don't want to hurt her and his daughters, but I don't want to be without him either. Can I share him and be okay? Do I want to continue subjecting my heart, body and soul to this evitable hurt and pain, but I don't want anyone else but him, no one else will do. He is…why? Why God, why was I allowed to experience him? As I write he is performing the wedding ceremony he was requested to do. I am confused I don't know what to think. He reads me the bible and talks to me about making good decisions and what's best for my children and me; however he has me in a relationship that is not healthy, and I in so deep that I don't know how to get out without suffering a massive heartache.

How can I compete with my mirror image?

Is he just selfish?

How can he not allow me to date other men?

He won't even hear of it.

Party Animal

*W*ell he's back from the wedding and now we can really just enjoy our time without any more interruptions. He decided that he wanted to see the night life so we got dressed and went downtown. We hadn't eaten dinner yet so we went to a local spot and got some Jerk chicken, the food of the island is good everywhere. After we ate we walked down the street to the Greenhouse. It was a nightclub, it was packed with people.

He turned up the alcohol since he doesn't have any more "Pastoral" duties to perform. He really had a great time, he was drinking Rum Runner's, and he was lit up. He can really dance. We danced, he drank, and we danced, and he drank. He was so lit up that he could barely walk. He did this bounce that he told me his youngest daughter taught him. There were so many people there, and him in his off white linen suit, and tipsy as he was, was not a good look – I felt like someone could have robbed us, he was totally out of pocket... so I flagged down a cop who called a friend of his that was a cab driver to come pick us up, and take us back to the hotel... I got him to bed – he got up at 4:30am and there he goes. He's baaack. Mr. Energizer bunny; from the moment he got to St. Thomas we did "it" 16 times, I could not believe this 52 year old had me hemmed up 16 times and was still ready. Huh, my 36 year old self needed a mid-day nap. He got it in 3 times before 10am every morning.

Eewwwh, I need a spare!

Day 5

"It was all a Dream?"

*I*t's time to go home, we had breakfast and everything was good, neither one of us are ready to come back home. Why can't we stay right here? Well, we are sitting together on the plane, he isn't happy about that though. He told me I should have taken a different flight back because the wedding party and guests would probably be on the same flight as us. Well, anyway I didn't listen to him and we flew home together. When we landed for our layover he checked his voicemail. He told me Mia called him and wanted to talk. Ut oh! I am nervous. I told her we were going away, I asked her not to say anything I wonder if she was about to tell him the things I told her? I am scared, my stomach is in knots. He tells me she calls and is wondering what she wants, he sees the look on my face and asked me what I did? He's angry. I told him she figured it out all on her own. He said I should have just lied and made her look like she was crazy and didn't know what she was talking about. I couldn't do that. She clearly told me that she saw it all over his face every time I walked in the room. She said, he would utter, "here comes my baby" and the only one in sight was me!

When we landed I took my luggage and went to my truck, once I was in my truck he called his wife and told her he had arrived and she came and picked him up from the airport.

Paradise was over!

14

Snap Back to Reality

What went wrong?

Overall we had a great time in St. Thomas, but since we've been home he has been on some next shit! The trip was to secure our relationship but somehow I feel like it made the situation worse. I am more insecure now than before we left. He said our relationship would not be the same, and I didn't know what that meant. I need to find a way out of this. He is causing me too much pain; I am on a constant rollercoaster. I wish Pastor Reed had just brought me in for counseling when this first happened and I reported it perhaps it would have stopped there. The Pastors at Sharon Baptist Church with the exception of Pastor Peterson are all a royal mess. He told me about the Bishop T.D. Jakes conference in July that all of the pastors had just come back from. He said one of his fellow pastors spent his time putting down Courvoisier, and that the other one was so drunk that he was sick vomiting and couldn't make it down to the meetings. He is the real "Party Pastor" cause he can handle his liquor and be functional the next day. He said that the only reason Pastor Reed hangs out with him is because his wife is "holiness", and doesn't allow him to smoke or drink in his own home. He will hang out with him for his "pleasure principal". Pastor Caines said his wife knows he is crazy. Damn him! I went to this Church to get my life together not get twisted by the Pastor, fall in love and get caught up!

It's a week later, I tossed and turned all night, I had a headache, I woke up twice to take Tylenol – It was Glenn, I prayed and asked God for help and Glenn called; God took my pain away. I can breathe again, Glenn called twice this morning, and we were fighting and making up at the same time. He told me he loves me and he loves me the best way he can in spite of the situation. He screamed about my $39,000.00 necklace. He told me he understands that shopping makes me feel better. He does not have to buy me diamonds just touch it. He told me about Pastor Lambert's fall from grace with his woman and about Pastor Reed's situation with the woman from the choir that they forced out of the church and sent to another Philadelphia church. There were times when Pastor Caines and I were together and he was calling his fellow comrades for an alibi for the day and they were calling him for the same. I realized this is what the Pastors do, it's a "Gentleman's Club."

I can still remember feeling tormented in my soul when I returned from St. Thomas, I'm like how can I go to church and listen to him preach and also listen to Bishop Reed preach, and talk about all these things that are convicting to my spirit, fully knowing that he still desires to be with me, because he still spoke to me in a very sexual manner. I just didn't understand that, at one point I even questioned if there was a God, because how could all these pastors stand here in the pulpit preaching about living right, and tithing, and all the things that honor God, but then they leave the church and have all these sexual escapades.

During the course of our relationship we talked about the preachers in the pulpit. We talked about his peers. He told me numerous stories of how he was living in Bermuda just a few years prior and Bishop Reed would come there and how he would have him set up with women on a consistent basis. He told me about all of Bishop Reed's sexual indiscretions and how the only reason that Pastor Caines is still employed is Sharon Baptist Church is because Bishop Reed would not fire him being knowledgeable of all the dirt. He called it his skeletons he knows where all his "bodies lay." He knows about the majority of women he has been with outside of his marriage, all the sexual indiscretions

Bishop Reed has had although he has been married for like 25 years to the same woman. Pastor Caines relationship with him goes back some 16 years now. Pastor Caines told me about other pastors within their organization that actually had sex with counselees in their office. He said that this was just the culture and that is why they were so comfortable with it.

Pastor Caines use to call and say he was my daddy. He also emailed me to say, "It's your Daddy" and "Who's your Daddy?" You're my daddy in a sexual sense but I got so caught up in this relationship. I was so caught up that I was literally going around telling people he was my daddy. I was telling people that he was my god-father and then I would have to back track and say, "My godfather is also my Pastor."

I told my friend from Maryland that Pastor Caines was my godfather and also my Pastor. He did not realize that my godfather who is also my pastor is the man who I had been in a relationship with. I was so twisted in my brain that I literally bought into the fact that Pastor Caines became my godfather and my spiritual accountability, but he was also the man that I was having sex with. How could I believe all of that garbage?

Spiritual accountability

Who was he "accountable to?

Caught up in a real mess!
I Don't Want to be Baptized

I am so angry with him right now. When I joined the church I signed up to be baptized although I had it done when I was 15 years old. I had gone through my 10 weeks of spiritual boot camp at the church and taking classes at the Biblical Institute. However, I told him a couple of days ago that I was not feeling getting baptized this Sunday, mainly because of our relationship. He said, "What are you feeling?"

"Allow the Lord to bless your life;

God is birthing something in you."

Now I am really confused…The look of Integrity in this man was off the chain. He had the nerve….

I decided to go with it, he then calls me Sunday morning at 7:45 am to tell me he would be there at the baptism, and he mentions nothing about his daughters being sick. He calls me back at 2:20 pm and leaves me a message telling me some !@#$ about his daughters not feeling well, being home alone and his son wanting to come by his house to talk with him. I feel like he is lying to me. All of a sudden he is being selective about what he is telling me now.

The same real estate client of mine that he introduced me to and we all went out to dinner afterwards got married yesterday, and he didn't even mention it to me. I am so angry. He is digging himself a 12 foot grave – he is going to wish he was 12 feet under if he hurts me or if I get hurt in this mess....Yes mess! God's word will come right back to swipe him.

I resent the fact that I am all caught up in this chaos and I cannot get myself out of it. I need to start dating; anything is worth the try to get away from Pastor Caines and this sinful relationship that is destroying me inside. He thinks he is helping me –

I am fighting a war inside of me.

He is feeding my flesh,

My emotions,

My mental state

He is feeding "My Everything...."

Pastor Reed preached today – he spoke about the Enemy transforming "More than meets the eye" and knowing what you like, fishing and putting the right type of bait on the hook. Glenn is definitely the "right bait" and the hook is in my throat, my friends cannot believe I am caught up! They all tell me how sorry they are for me. I have had cosmetic surgery because he wanted me to. Even though I was unsure about the procedure he talked me right into it.

He has told me that he will never leave his wife, that he is committed to her and that commitment keeps him there. He asks me why I would want to be with someone who leaves his wife and kids for them. I'm asking myself the same thing.

He is prepared (emotionally) for me to leave him;

He said he is a "realist."

He knows that he has control over me and my emotions and I can't just walk away from him.

He is good at the mind games.

Thank God business is good right now; I am making a ton of money in the real estate business. A client of mine bought me two dozen roses, and another gave me a huge bonus for doing the deal.

I left my real estate broker of almost three years abruptly because of his insensitivity. I have had enough and I will probably leave Glenn the same way, abruptly! Huh, I am in the process of setting up an account to allow Glenn to make some money since as he states he is struggling. He is really feeling himself. He constantly reminds me that I make more money than he and his wife put together huh, he could care less if I walked out of his life.

It was the *E*xperience he says.

.

15

"His Wife is Sleeping in "My" Bed"

*I*n September of 2006, I moved out of the house I had rented because that house was up for foreclosure; the landlord has abandoned it. So I ended up finding a house and purchasing it. Since I was buying a much larger home I bought all new bedroom furniture for me and my children. I emailed pastor Caines and asked him to put up a bulletin in the church that I was giving furniture away to families who needed it. We were just upgrading.

Read the email and guess what happens next?

Furniture

Tuesday, November 14, 2006 1:04 PM
From:
"Shannon R. Bellamy"
To:
"K.Glenn Caines"

Good afternoon Pastor Caines,

I would like to give you and your family the first opportunity of some bedroom furniture I would like to bless someone with. I have three girls' twin size bed frames that have a white decorative head and footboard with decorative balls on each post, in addition to 2 white nightstands, a white and pink dress with a desk attachment, two twin size mattress and box springs. Please let me know if your family or anyone else may be interested. Also, I have a queen size bedroom set with a dresser/mirror, headboard mirror, chest drawers and nightstand and entertainment center as well. The items must be picked up this week.

God Bless and Take care
Shannon Bellamy

ell, Pastor Caines said he needed it. He brought his wife to my house. He had just left my house the day before for our weekly "session".

He brings his wife to my house to look at furniture and his wife picked out "my" bedroom furniture. So currently in his house right now he has my bedroom furniture, the furniture we had been on together. He has my bedroom furniture in his house! He has two of my mirrors in his house. He has my dresser, the mirror to the dresser, and a wall unit that I had in my bedroom. He came to my house as the Pastor, to come and show his wife this furniture that they were getting "blessed" with for free from a "parishioner." However, he had just left there the day before, boy is he slick! I cannot believe my eyes; he got a set of balls on him! I felt like a sheep among a mighty wolf!

What was I to say? He pranced around my home with her, all "lovie dovie". I was angry, the nerve of him I thought. I will not let him damper this exciting time for my children and me. We are moving in to a 5 bedroom home with a 20x40 in-ground pool, basement, and office and entertainment room. I did it with only the help of my Aunt and God the Father; Daddy Glenn… and with my own money.

My children and I moved into our house by ourselves. It's okay because we did it as a family, it was hard work. I have always told my children...

You Work hard and Play even harder!

I don't apologize for the abundance God has given us because I have worked my butt off to get it. No matter how difficult times were I always got up and found a way to make "it" happen. "It" being whatever I needed to, to ensure a great and comfortable life for my children and me.

At this time Pastor Caines had stopped me from physically going to his office for counseling but he continued to counsel me over the phone and at my home. We talked on the phone everyday – eight to nine times per day. It was either him calling me, or me calling him on our cell phones, as well as the church phones.

Once we were in the new house he would come over whenever his wife would leave town, he never spent the night at my house because he wanted to be home to answer the phone in case she called during the night. However, by day break he was already at my house, and in my bed. After having spent some quality time with me he would go on with his day from there.

We would meet – at this point he was teaching classes. He was teaching a class on "Overview of Bible Doctrines" and I was one of his students. This was at Sharon

Baptist Biblical Institute. I took two classes with him – two semesters. After class we would go have dinner. We would have a "special" rendezvous, sometimes after class as well. We would leave church and a lot of times we would meet at the Hilton Airport Hotel. We would never go to the hotel for a room; we were always either in my truck, his truck or basically at my house. Ninety percent of the time it was at my house. But after church we would normally meet and we would go down to the restaurant in the hotel and sit there and have dinner and cocktails before he went home.

We would have breakfast during the week together before he had to go to work. We usually would have breakfast at the Penrose Diner. We would also go out to lunch. I would buy food and we would have picnics, and we would just meet anywhere. We would meet at a parking lot near church and we would sit out there and have lunch if he did not have enough time to come to my house. On the weekends, if he had a church meeting to go to, he would come to my house after the church meeting. He would do whatever he had to do for the church in the morning and then come to my house for a couple of hours before going home. Or he would come and see me after he would get a haircut on a Saturday morning before anybody at home realized that he has been gone too long. This was consistent. He went with me and my kids to school as well when they had problems.

16

"Just When I thought Everything was Great"

O n January 6, 2007 my life would forever change. I was out with my daughter and a friend, and while we were driving back from dinner I received a phone call from the Wilmington police department stating Kent Davis was under arrest for armed robbery. I said, "So, why are you calling me?" The police officer said because he asked to contact you, "why, we are not together", I replied. He said, because he is a minor. Oh my god, I thought they were talking about my son's father, but they were actually talking about my son! I almost flipped my truck over; I liked to have fainted from the news. I later find out that my son and some other people had gotten into a mess of trouble. To make a long story short my son spent four months in juvenile detention. While there he wrote a letter to Pastor Caines, asking him to come and visit him. On one Sunday afternoon after church Pastor Caines and his wife drove down to see my son. As usual I was there, because I never missed any of the visitations with my son. Pastor Caines wife was not able to go in; therefore, she drove around for the 2 hours he was there. She and I made small talk; I was nice but not very friendly. I was shocked that she was there. I guess she didn't trust him after all.

Then around...I would say around January of 2007, I was talking about how uncomfortable I was with my stomach, and he suggested that I have a tummy tuck done.

Back around April, after we had sex the first time, he asked me if I was on birth control - after the fact. I told him no. He told me that I need to get on birth control pills. I had not taken birth control pills for three years at this point. I had been on them for a long time and I knew that it could become dangerous if you are on them for a long time at my age so I wanted to give my body a break.

He told me to get back on birth control pills because he didn't want to use condoms and he thought that the birth control pill was the best thing for me to get. At his advice, I went to the doctor and got birth control pills. Subsequently, like I said, I had gotten pregnant the year before by my husband.

Back to what I was saying, now came the talks about my stomach. I was uncomfortable with my stomach so I inquired about having a tummy tuck. He immediately said yes do it. I was contemplating it. I was unsure because it was a major surgery. I hadn't had any complications with the breast augmentation, he said do it, I will be right there. I had the surgery scheduled the same week Pastor Reed had his 50th birthday celebration and was becoming Bishop. What a spectacle that was. Pastor Caines told me he had no intentions of participating in the festivities. He and Pastor Caines had a love hate toxic relationship. Pastor Caines told me that when Pastor Reed went to become Bishop that women came out of the woodwork about his infidelity with them. Pastor Caines said he wrote a letter to the head of the Bishop Counsel for Pastor Reed smoothing things over for him to become Bishop. He said Pastor Reed becoming Bishop would allow him to get 10% from the churches he is over every year in a "love offering" to him. Pastor Caines wrote the letter, he is a great and persuasive writer and Pastor Keith W. Reed Sr. is now Bishop Keith W. Reed Sr.

I could not believe that he became Bishop; I thought Bishop's were beyond the petty sins that the parishioners in the pews go through. I know bigger lever bigger devil, but Bishop Reed's indiscretions costs him a lot of members and the respect of many. It's sad, but as I was preparing to release this book, people were in suspense about which church it was, and every single person guessed it right!

Now that is a Shame!

Pastor Caines is feeling a "sista'" right about now...read his email to me...FYI...3955 is the address of the church:

Just Because

Saturday, February 3, 2007 2:41 PM
From:
"Kenneth Caines"
To:
Shannonrbellamy

Yesterday was wonderful on many fronts.

The time of heartfelt sharing was not wasted. I have taken what you said to my heart, and you even more into my heart.

To watch you handle your business at #23 Highwoods was a pleasure to observe.

The moments in the serene place was "Another Again". As usual the time was impeccable and the impact emotionally and physically was superb.

By the way after I left, I began to on I-76 West on my way to the church and decided it would cast a shadow on my mood and aura...3955 was given the fly by. I After I spoke with you came home settled with a glass of Merlot and reflected.

Once again I saw you, I saw me, I saw us and we were beautiful...Another Again.

Today I've talked to you twice (so far), but thought of you continuously...thanks for being you.

As promised I'm sending the drinks website www.drinksmixer.com it's a great resource for my ultimate hostess with the mostest...

Holla...Just Because

17

"The Power of the Blood"

I went back to Dr. Lo to discuss the procedure, it would be in excess of $10,000 for the tummy tuck and liposuction, I had already spent $6,000 for the breast augmentation.

Things with Pastor Caines and I are pretty wishy washy by now, and I am attempting to start over, and be social with other people.

At the end of March I made a friend in Maryland. I told Pastor Caines about this man, he was furious. I told him that I needed a companion for myself. He acted like I was committing a crime for wanting to spend time with someone other than him, but I was trying to break away from the hold he had on me. I remember meeting Travis on my favorite website "Blackpeoplemeet." I rejoined without Pastor Caines' knowledge. He and I talked on the phone for a while, one afternoon I decided to drive to Maryland for a day trip with my daughters. Since I knew he had daughters as well, I invited him to a family date on the Marina with our girls. The day was perfect, we met, he was more beautiful than his pictures I thought, and he had a strong English accent, 6'2 and nice solid body type with a bald head and goatee. He was born and raised in England and his parents were from Sierra Leone Hill in West Africa. He is a very spiritual man. He went to a great church in Maryland that I later attended to see him perform in the theatrical production for Easter.

On our family date we strolled the Marina and Art Gallery with our daughters, paddle boated, went to the Aquarium and had dinner at the Cheesecake Factory. It was a perfect afternoon. I started spending more time in Maryland. Travis and I would sleep in the same bed but that is it, just sleep. He was a perfect gentleman. My favorite time there was in the morning. He had a house larger and more beautiful than mine, he would get up in the morning, shower and shave and while I was sleeping he would make coffee, he would say "Darling would you like some coffee?" with that beautiful strong English accent of his, and I could just melt. Wow, what would I give to be his wife? I didn't feel worthy although I felt like royalty when I was with him. Travis has taken me to some of the most beautiful and exclusive restaurants in Maryland.

A couple of weeks later I told him that I was having a tummy tuck. He tried to convince me that I didn't need the surgery but I was not strong enough to tell Pastor Caines I wasn't going to do it. I was scared and torn about what to do.

Needless to say Pastor Caines won and on May 14, 2007, I had the procedure done.

After all of that Pastor Caines was not even there when I had the surgery, he was mad because I was talking to Travis. Travis was under the weather when I had the surgery and could not be there as well. My girlfriend brought me home after the procedure. After the procedure I was at home recuperating. I wasn't walking much because of the pain and the tightness of my stomach muscles.

All of a sudden 36 hours later around 1:00 am my heart started beating 120 beats a minute, I could literally hear it as if it was beating out loud for everyone to hear. I called my girlfriend Camille who works for my OB/GYN and told her what I was experiencing. While I was talking with her it felt like someone had stabbed me in my chest. She said call Dr. Lo right away. I called Dr. Lo and told him and he said go to the hospital right away.

Now I am nervous! I screamed, woke up my children and told them to call 911 and hit the buttons on the alarm system. I was afraid; I didn't know what was happening.

Thirty-six hours after I had the tummy tuck....

I was rushed to the emergency room by the Ambulance!

When I arrived at the Cooper University Hospital in Camden they immediately checked my incision and then sent me for an x-ray. The x-ray came back fine. Something is wrong, they checked my pulse and said send her to CAT scan STAT. I was wheeled down to the CAT scan room and the technician said to me lay flat on your back. I said I couldn't because I had just been cut from hip to hip. The technician said fine, send her back to her room. On my way back to the ER room the doctor saw me and the transporter asked him if I was done already, when he told the doctor that the technician said to send me back to my room because I wouldn't lay flat, he was livid. He said, "Ms. Bellamy you need this test, if it is what I think, this test will save your life". The Doctor the called CAT scan technician and said get a nurse to give me morphine if I needed it for the pain, but I want her to have this test STAT! The transporter wheeled me back to the CAT scan and I slowly tolerated the pain and laid on the table for the test without getting the morphine. Before the transporter and I could get back to ER room the ER doctor had the report. About five minutes after I arrived back to my bed the ER doctor and four other doctors came into the room and stood around me. They were looking at me strangely. I start crying. I said what, what is it? The doctor said,

"You have bilateral pulmonary embolism"!

"What is that, I asked?"

"You have several blood clots in both your lungs and a major one in your right lung."

I said, "Why are so many doctors in here", he said they are marveled that you are still alive, I said, "get my kids out of here and someone call my mother." The doctor went on to say **Pulmonary embolism** (PE) is a common and potentially lethal condition that can cause death in all age groups.

1 in 10 people die within the first hour.

The PE was caused by a combination of the birth control pills and the tummy tuck. I would not have had either one if it were not for my supportive Pastor!

Immediately the lab techs come in my room and hook up IV's in both my arms. They started working on me right away, trying to safe my life. I did not understand, my heart was beating a little fast and my incision a little sore but otherwise I felt fine. "What do you mean; we are trying to save your life", I asked the doctor?

I was in ICU for seven days and in the hospital for three weeks. The doctor explained that because of the major abdominal surgery I had undergone they could not put a filter in me to stop the blot clots from traveling. He said all they could do is thin my blood, to almost a water consistency. He explained that your body has the ability to break down the blood clots on its own, but my body has to want to fight to live and repair itself, the only help they could be was to thin my blood so that the clots could flow freely without obstructing anything.

I was wheeled to the Intensive Care Unit.

The Power of the Blood!

After being in ICU for a couple of hours a patient in the room next to me Died! You mean to tell me, the grim reaper is walking around on this floor?

The birth control pills caused the blood clots in my leg; the abdominal surgery has a major clotting factor as well. No more birth control for me. I was admitted into the Intensive Care Unit at the Hospital. I come out of the hospital after being there for about three to four weeks and now I'm on blood thinners for six months. Pastor Caines knows at this point that he must do something about the birth control issue.

Now I have to go to the doctor twice per week to make sure my blood is thinned out appropriately. When I went to my OB/GYN and told them what had happened she suggested that I do the IUD. The IUD is for the monogamous couple. IUD means Intrauterine Device. I told Pastor Caines that the doctor said I can get the IUD because it has no hormones, but it is for monogamous couples. If a person had more than one sex partner, and they are on it, they can get sick from it. It can cause pelvic infections and cause one to get severely sick. I explained that to him, and then told him I would get the IUD, conditionally. I informed him of the warnings and potential danger with this device and asked him that he not put me at risk.

18

"Boxing Day"

t some point I believe Pastor Caines' wife starting having suspicions about our relationship, particularly since she invited me and my children over to their home for Boxing Day (aka the day after Christmas). I felt that was strange because we rarely spoke and had gone out to dinner only once previously, and that was in a group setting.

So I was puzzled as to why she had invited me and my children to a family event of theirs especially during the holiday season. Nevertheless, I decided to accept the invitation and we reluctantly went. My children were excited, but I myself had a cold that day and wasn't feeling particularly well. I found a seat in the kitchen and sat there all night thinking that was where all the women would be congregating. To my surprise, she was all over the house entertaining, while Pastor Caines stayed in the kitchen dishing out food. His father-in-law and I had some great intellectual conversations; however his mother-in-law came into the room and shut that down. Later I find out by Pastor Caines that his mother-in-law told his wife in front of him to "watch out for her, she wants your husband", huh, little did she know her daughters' husband wanted me!

19

"You Get What You Get!"

*I*n January 2008, I was on the IUD and I had sex with him on a Monday and then had sex with him the following Thursday. In between Monday and Thursday he had sex with his wife. On Friday I called him and said,

- ❖ "Did you have sex with your wife this week?"
- ❖ He said, "Why are asking me about what goes on in my house"
- ❖ I said to him, "Have I ever questioned you about your business?"
- ❖ I said, "I am asking you for a reason."
- ❖ He said "Yes, I had sex with my wife."
- ❖ I told him I know because "I'm sick now."
- ❖ I was angry. I said, "I went to the doctor. "
- ❖ I said, "Didn't I ask you not to put me at risk?"
- ❖ **I said, "You disgust me, you make me sick!"**
- ❖ And he said to me,

❖ "Well, you get what you get."

Basically, you're the whore. I'm not his wife. I'm the one he's having an affair with. So you get what you get, like I was dirty and deserved it. I was angry by that statement.

❖ I was done; the Rose colored glasses had been shattered!

Now I can see who he truly is and that it was all trickery. For months he tried to get me back into that life of sin with him. He said, "I lost my way". How is it your Pastor who preaches weekly, counsels daily, knows the Bible back and forth, teaches the Word of God daily can lose his way by the end of night and conveniently find it in time to "go to work" in the morning?

My faith, my heart, my soul was shattered. I didn't even know if I could love someone else again. I didn't talk about it to no one. I sincerely repented and I prayed continuously everyday to Christ to not let me feel the pain of not having him in my life anymore. I promised God that if he doesn't allow me to feel the pain I would never go back down that road of sin ever again with Pastor Caines and I meant it. I am not scorned. I am not mad he didn't leave his wife. I have never felt hate, pain, sorrow or urned for Pastor Caines not being in my life after January 2008. God kept up his side and never allowed my heart to ache for him. I am healed.... thanks to Christ! God spared by life and he has only asked that I come forward and share my story with others in hope to give them strength to deliver themselves from the same situations, that is the very least I can do. They talked about Christ and he was perfect! He gave my children their mother back stronger, healthier and wiser. He didn't take my life when the doctor's said they couldn't do anything for else for me. He answered my prayers, for this I am eternally grateful and give him all the Honor and the Glory!

Be Blessed!

Be Inspired!

"Knowledge is Power!"

oo many churches see the victims of sexual exploitation by predatorial pastors as "just rewards" for women (and occasionally men) that have not been able to defend their sexual boundaries when it is invaded by some helper in authority over them. Too often, our church leaders call these criminal acts "an affair" -- and blame the counselee for being "equally responsible" -- in most states sexual exploitation by helping professionals is criminal sexual conduct in the third degree -- a felony!

It is disgraceful even to speak of wicked things done in secret; however that exposure drags dark deeds into the light, waking "sleeping" believers that they in turn might walk wisely. I decided to write this book because I needed to release myself from the blame of this inappropriate relationship. The Bible says in John 8:32 "Then you will know the truth, and the truth will set you free." That applies to all of us. Now he is free, I am free and the future unsuspecting women are free.

Sexual contact during or after any counseling relationship is considered grossly unethical by a broad slice of professional counseling groups, including the American Association of Christian Counselors, the American Association of Pastoral Counselors, and the National Association of Social Workers. That's because of the power counselors hold over clients—power born of authority and being privy to clients' most intimate emotions and fears. Experts say this power is magnified in pastoral counseling.

"The counselee often sees the minister not only as a professional with her best interests at heart, but also at times as the very instrument of God's healing power, and possibly as her last refuge of hope."

It seems God's judgment is public and shameful upon them all and all invitations to date encouraging their repentance are met with silence. When a pastor steals that hope by sexualizing a counseling relationship, damage to women can range from depression to relationship trouble to suicide, said Gary Schoener, a Minneapolis psychologist who has consulted in more than 3,000 clergy sexual abuse (CSA) cases since 1980.

Two prominent evangelical Christians, Peter Mosgofian and George Ohlschlager published a book in

1995 ("Sexual Misconduct in Counseling and Ministry") warning that sexual predators in the ministry and other helping professions is one of the major social problems in our nation today. The following stories explain why sexual contact between a counselor and counselee is NEVER consensual, NEVER an "affair." Peter warned the early church of "false teachers" who "seduce the unstable ... entice by sensual passions of the flesh," who promise freedom while "they themselves are slaves of corruption.

Author, Shannon Bellamy

Your Perception… is Your Reality

Where am I now?

I was confused and the relationship certainly caused me to be consistently warring between my flesh and spirit, at this point I am numb when it comes to attending church.

I know all Pastors are all not the same and many are dedicated to enriching the lives of people and making a positive impact in their life. I am working toward re-building my spiritual life. I am consistently watching Joel Osteen on Sunday's and allowing God to speak to me through him and my own prayer life. I thank God for the Pastors that are truly dedicated to their ministry and not their "job".

Everyday I don't think about or call my former Counselor, Friend, Confidant and former Lover who is "Her" Husband," Their Father" and my former "Pastor" is a good day. God has removed that stronghold he had over my life. God has set me free and I am whole.

To God be the Glory, It is my prayer that there will come a change in the method in which counseling is being conducted in the churches to prevent the Pastors and Counselors from engaging in inappropriate relationships with their counselees.

No matter what you've done or what you're going through, you are not alone. There are other women just like you, and through God's grace and mercy they have been restored. God wants you to know that He loves you with an everlasting, unconditional love and you cannot change that. He has a wonderful plan for your life and desires to see you happy and prosperous. All it requires is that you believe and want it. You have a voice....

Break the Silence and ….. Begin to Live!

Thank you for touching my life.....

my guardian angels

To my favorite cousin Joel "Pumpkin" Walker what can I say I love you and thank you for your support and for making this project a priority, I appreciate you, your time and your talents; to my friend Wanda thank you for 22 years of true and sincere friendship and always "clutching your Pearls", Trina Stackhouse thank you for taking me under your wing and helping me birth this "baby"! Liz thank you for always telling the truth and introducing me to the NY style woman, Vanessa thank you for your support and unconditional friendship even when you didn't agree with my "choices", Camille thank you for always having something positive to say and never getting frustrated with all of the calls over the last 21 years and being a great ear, Roxanne thank you for the 16 years of friendship and always making me feel welcome whenever I came around , Tanya it has been a real pleasure and I thank you for your honesty and friendship and never judging me, Pam girl thank you for the 24 years of friendship and for always making me feel like I got it all together, Bernice what can I say for the last 30 years you have been by my side even when I made it difficult for you, Teliah thank you for being the sister who never complained about life; you just picked up your kids and moved; you were never afraid of change and I celebrate you, Mom thank you for giving me life and caring for me when I was on the brink of death after my cosmetic surgery procedure, Sheila girl thank you for 19 years of friendship and always being ready to "roll-out" without question, Vicki thank you for 21 years of friendship and showing me it's never too late to finish school, Dennis thank you for supporting me and for allowing God to use you and show me unconditional friendship and love, you were in my life for a season and I am blessed for that, it's because of your character and core values that helped me to break away from the mental and spiritual deception I was living, thank you for standards and always treating me with respect. Richard Crosby thank you for being my friend and a mentor to my son, you have been a great example of what God can do if you keep your heart focused on him. Zahyid you have been a real Guardian Angel, thank you for your friendship and support you'll always be my "lil' dude", Jack Harris thank you for your core values, support and mentoring; I know everything I do about real estate because of you, Jeff Harris, my buddy, thank you for being like a big brother to me and being a true friend and mentor to my children and thank you for always being honest with me; Art thank you for being my friend and "Mr. Give Me Hard Time" and allowing me to be free to be me without reservation and for encouraging and believing in me and being such a positive and disciplined addition to my life, I love you; T.I. thank you for being my business partner, my brother and my friend, and being business savvy and believing in me most of all introducing me to Art, who has captured my heart in such a sweet and tender way and Lorrisa thank you for sharing your man Gurl :o) for business and not complaining when we were up late at night on the phone building my empire, John Barber it really means a lot to me that you have been so supportive I really appreciate you and all that you have done, Sean "Dakota" Anderson thank you for being a great friend, supporting me and keeping me grounded, Miles thank you for believing in me and your unconditional friendship and supporting this endeavor, Uncle Booker thank you for believing in me and being there for me and my children, Uncle Larry thank you for showing me it's okay to want to be a Chef and a Lawyer and you're never too old to do it. Uncle John thank you for the best childhood memories, Aunt Peggie thank you for sacrificing for me and my children, I will always love you for what you did for us, Aunt Nancy thank you for loving me and my children from the day I found you and treating us like we've been in your life for our entire lives, my daddy would be proud to know that you have loved his only daughter unconditionally and welcomed her into the Bellamy family with open arms, Aunt Nancy thank you for taking the time to spend time talking about daddy and bringing him alive to me and allowing me to get to know my daddy through your eyes, I love you. Baby brother D it's all good, we are just alike and daddy would be proud, "You already know". Grandma Bellamy thank you for giving me one of the greatest memories I could ever have, you baking me a cake when I met you for the very first time when I turned 33 years old and loving me instantly and sharing your memories of my daddy with me. To my Nana it's because of you I am the wonder woman I am today, thank you for your strength, teaching me to cook, for my elite domestication skills (smile) and Sophistication, you will always be my #1 Girl, thank you for the sweet memories R.I.P.

Special Thanks

God Who is the Head of My Life
My children
Trina Stackhouse
Joel B. Walker
Ericka Williams
Kamal Imani
Lila Ntumba
Earl Groom Jr.
Ultimate Body Image
Business in the Black Web design
John Barber III Come Kleen Productions
Tim Whiteside Sang Entertainment
Solomon Williams Kat in the Hat Entertainment
Robert "Big Press" Presbury
Barbara Sheree
Buck Wild
DJ Lisa Love
Rabiyah
Wali Hamid
Simon Carr Punchline Apparel
Stephanie Cain of Cain Productions
Ed & Lydia Ward III of Ward Legacy Productions
In Full Bloom by Rolanda Chung
Jerry's Carpet Store
South Jersey Printing
Chase Design and Print
Michelle Shane Infinity Publishing
*
Suite 215
Art Carr, Jonett D'Veauxbray, Ericka Glenn & Shekhinah B
Tobijah Anderson T.I.A Entertainment
*

A message from the author…

"The Spirit of the Lord GOD is upon me; because the LORD hath anointed me to preach good tidings unto the meek; he hath sent me to bind up the brokenhearted, to proclaim liberty to the captives, and the opening of the prison to them that are bound…to comfort all that mourn…to give unto them beauty for ashes, the oil of joy for mourning, the garment of praise for the spirit of heaviness…For your shame ye shall have double; and for confusion they shall rejoice in their portion…" *(read entire passage)* Isaiah 61:1-7 KJV

I am fearfully and wonderfully made; Wonderful are Your works, And my soul knows it very well. Psalms 139:14 NASB

Chase your dreams…
it loves the Pursuit

"To my children who are the loves of my life."

To my son I am so proud of you and I am grateful that God gave you to me first, you are a Man, be proud and responsible – you are an Eagle never forget! To my daughters…so full of character, spice, mental wit, curiosity and beauty thank you for being my #1 fans, looking up to me , admiring me and always filling my heart with love. You make me want to do better every day because I know you're watching and learning from me. You are your mother's children and I love you all with every breath in my body. You are all a true and divine blessing from God! Your mom is not perfect however, it is my heart's desire to give you a happy, healthy, exciting, disciplined and God centered life with lots of love and nurturing Make me proud and leave an impression in your lifetime for those to come! Remember you can be whatever your heart desires, and when your desire changes, its okay just Reposition yourself!

"Letter to the Church"

God has placed a charge on His elect to care for the lost children of the world, but many have grossly abused the privilege and stewardship of this Christ given authority. I pray that there will be lessons learned from Shannon's experience that will help others who find themselves in similar situations. Never compromise your integrity or character for mere moments of pleasure, so that your walk may be in keeping with the principles of the word of God. Nothing can offer the fulfillment of life as completely as the word of God can, and true fulfillment in anything can never be realized if *God* is not a part of the equation. I also pray that if there were only one good that could come from the authors' experience that it would be SAME SEX COUNSELING, or at the very least 'Pastor assisted counseling', which I firmly believe would seriously diminish much of the indiscretions that occur when men of the clergy counsel women. May God bless you, and may heaven smile upon you!

Joel B. Walker

Bishop Edward Brink

I am very proud of you for exposing Sexual immorality in the pulpit. One of the reasons why we don't see the Power and Glory of God in Our Churches Today is because of Sexual Immorality and Unclean spirits operating in the Church World today. I Thank God that I've been Married and am still Married to my First Wife of 17 Years this November 2009. I am 44 Years old and in Ministry for over 20 Years. It is my Prayer that God Prospers and Blesses you in this project.

Best Regards.
Co-Worker in the Gospel of Jesus Christ.
Bishop Edward Brink

Apostle L.R. Jackson III

WOMAN OF GOD-
Be Thou Excited, because God has brought you out and is taking you Higher in Him.

Apostle L.R. Jackson III

You can contact Shannon Bellamy
to request speaking engagements
through:

Shannon Bellamy Enterprises
P.O. Box 853
Sicklerville, NJ 08081

~Or~

Phone: 201-759-8561
info@shannonbellamy.com

~Or~

Web site:

www.shannonbellamy.com
www.pimpsinthepulpit-thebook.com

Upcoming Titles by the Best Selling Author Shannon Bellamy

"*Breaking the Silence*"

"*Triumph*"
Memoirs of a True Diva

"*You're his Wife...But I'm His Woman*"

"*Internet Dating*"

"*Snap - Look what you made me do*"

And the long awaited cookbook
"*Cooking with Shannon Bellamy*".

References

Personality & Tempermant Test (Oneishy, 2009)

biblestudytools.com/NAS

En.wikipedia.org/wiki/four_temperments

Womanbygrace.com/Christian-life/choleric-personalitytype

Perry, Tyler – Madea Goes to Jail t-shirt (2005)

Apostle Greenup, Louis S. "How to Stop the Other Woman from Stealing Your Husband"

http://www.biblegateway.com/passage/Isaiah61:1-7

http://www.biblegateway.com/passage/Psalms139:14

http://www.peacemakers.net/clergysexualabuse/protestants facesexabuse.htm

Mosgofian, P.; Ohlschlager, G. "Sexual Misconduct in Counseling and Ministry", 1995

http:// www.blackpeoplemeet.com

Shannon R. Bellamy